THE MEN

OF

HMS VICTORY

AT TRAFALGAR

including

THE MUSTER ROLL OF HMS VICTORY

Casualties, Parliamentary Grant, Prize Money

Lloyd's Patriotic Fund Rewards

Medals, Pay Rates

John D. Clarke

VINTAGE NAVAL LIBRARY

Nelson in the uniform of a Rear Admiral.
He is wearing the decorations of:
The most Honourable Order of the Bath. The Order of the Great Cross of St. Ferdinand and Merit, from the King of Naples. Imperial Crescent, from the Grand Seignior of the Ottoman Empire, Selim the Third. Three gold medals are worn, one of which is the Naval Large Gold Medal awarded for the Battle of the Nile, 1798.
Nelson's hat is adorned with a diamond aigrette, or plume of triumph, known as the 'Chelengk', a personal award from the Grand Seignior, for Nelson's victory at the Nile.

Also by JOHN D. CLARKE
Gallantry Medals & Awards of the World

Printed and bound by Antony Rowe Ltd, Eastbourne

CONTENTS

Introduction 7

Parliamentary Grant, Naval prize monies and pay 9

Ranks, their duties and clothing 14

History of Lloyd's Patriotic Fund and the awards 20

Illustration of Patriotic Fund swords, values £30, £50 & £100 25

Muster Roll of men serving on *Victory* at Trafalgar 26

List of men killed and wounded on *Victory* at Trafalgar 51

Death of Nelson and some of the personalities present 60

Lloyd's Patriotic Fund swords and vases awarded for Trafalgar 62

Naval Gold Medals awarded for Trafalgar 64

Naval General Service Medals awarded for Trafalgar 66

Privately awarded medals for Trafalgar 73

Ships under the command of Lord Nelson at Trafalgar 75

French and Spanish ships and their Captains at Trafalgar 76

Prisoners of war on board *Victory* 77

Biographical notes on crew members of *Victory* 78

References and acknowledgements 87

INTRODUCTION

HMS VICTORY

A TRUE MUSTER ROLL FOR 21st OCTOBER 1805

The Battle of Trafalgar and the part played by Vice-Admiral Lord Nelson's flagship *HMS Victory* has always stirred emotive feelings, not least among those who have an interest in Naval history and tradition. The research and compilation for this work has been undertaken with the intention of setting out a true roll, confirming all the officers and men who served on board *Victory*, during that victorious and decisive naval battle of 21 October 1805.

Forming this roll of *Victory's* crew at Trafalgar, necessitated checking that every man was mustered on board the flagship for pay and/or victuals for the four days leading up to and including the 21st October 1805. The reason that such a narrow band of time was selected as confirmation of service, was that prior to the naval battle, much activity had taken place within the fleet, which had included movement of personnel to and from the *Victory*.

After *Victory* arrived at Gibraltar on the 29th October, it was necessary that the ship's Muster Table should be calculated and approved for the period running from 1st September until 31st October 1805. Captain Hardy knew how important it was to confirm as a true record, all those men who had served on board during the period of the battle. He ordered his seven remaining lieutenants to attend the signing of the Muster Table, these officers were instructed to add their signatures below that of Captain Hardy.

At this historic signing, brave Lieutenant Pasco was suffering from frightful grape-shot wounds to his right arm and side, even so he was required to attend and place his signature to the document. Pasco in great pain made such a poor attempt at penning his name with his left hand, that the clerk was instructed to add a memo beside Pasco's signature explaining, "Written with his left hand, being wounded in the right arm." Such was the importance placed on having this document correct and accountable. Two lieutenants of the flagship did not sign this muster record, one was William Ram who was killed during the action, the other was George Miller Bligh, he had been struck in the head by a musket ball and was too ill to attend the signing.

Each man appearing in the foregoing roll has been checked to confirm his presence on board *Victory* for continuous service between the dates of 17th and the 24th of October 1805. In the original Muster book those who were "Killed in Action" had a line drawn through their muster date from the day they were buried at sea. Those who were mortally wounded but lingered on for a few days after the battle, like Landsman Henry Cramwell who died of his wounds and was buried at sea on the 26th October, had his wages and victuals paid for the period ending 24th October 1805.

Having arrived at a true roll, it then became possible to set out a listing of the Trafalgar battle casualties and the later rewards received by the men. I have attempted in the following pages to record details of how a nation rewarded its naval heroes for their part in Britain's greatest naval victory, the Battle of Trafalgar. The casualty roll of men listed in these pages, exceeds in number the casualties appearing in the original Admiralty despatches and other lists, the reason for that has been detailed in the section dealing with killed and wounded.

The monetry rewards gained by the men who had served on *Victory* during the battle, has been set out in table form, to include: Naval prize monies, the Parliamentary grant and the post Trafalgar enhanced pay rates.
Details of Lloyd's Patriotic Fund monetry awards for the injured are taken from the Lloyd's report of 1806. The wounded men are noted by rank and the seriousness of the type of wound they sustained in the battle, all of which reflected on the amount they were to receive from the Patriotic Fund Committee. The Lloyd's Patriotic Fund awards of swords and vases for the Trafalgar recipients and their relatives, have been detailed and illustrated, this information was kindly supplied by Lloyd's of London. The section on medals includes the roll of Naval Gold Medals, Large and Small, awarded to all who served in the fleet at Trafalgar. An updated Naval General Service Medal roll for the crew of *Victory*, has expanded details on the recipients and some sale room notes. The privately awarded medals of Boulton and Davison for the Battle of Trafalgar are described.

Included is a section detailing the duties and responsibilities of the various ranks and trades of the men on board the flagship, together with a section describing details of the type of clothing worn by men of the lower deck in 1805. Biographical notes on some sixty two officers and men who served on *Victory* during the battle of Trafalgar, plus notes on three officers who claimed to have served on the flagship, have been included. These details give an insight into how their lives were changed by Trafalgar.

It has been said over the years, that if every person who claimed to have served with Lord Nelson on *Victory* at the Battle of Trafalgar, was to be believed, the gallant ship would have sunk through the sheer weight of crew numbers. This compilation of names, casualties and rewards, will I hope enable those interested for family or historical reasons, to be able to confirm with some degree of certainty those sailors who served on *Victory* at the Battle of Trafalgar.

PARLIAMENTARY GRANT, NAVAL PRIZE MONIES AND PAY

Parliament on behalf of a grateful nation, voted a special grant of £300,000 to be divided amongst all the men of Nelson's victorious fleet. The officers and men engaged at the battle of Trafalgar also gained entitlement to the traditional naval prize money for the capture of enemy ships, the prize money allotted to any HMS ship was divided according to rank, in the manner set out below:

A. The Captain taking three eighths of the total prize money.
B. Captain of Marines, Sea Lieutenants and Masters shared another eighth.
C. Pursers, Gunners, Boatswains, Surgeons, Master's Mates and Lieutenants of Marines shared another eighth divided between them.
D. Midshipmen, Surgeon's Mates, Gunner's Mates, Sergeants of Marines, Petty Officers and Boatswain's Mates took a further eighth divided between them.
E. With the final quarter being shared amongst the rest of the crew and marines.

In this instance the prize money was quite substantial, the decisive engagement of Trafalgar had led to the capture of some fine and well built French and Spanish ships of war, some of these captured ships after repairs were to give sterling service to the British Navy. In the case of the captured French line-of-battle ship *Duguay Trouin*, she was taken into service and renamed *HMS Implacable*.

The *Implacable* would have survived until today had not the Admiralty wanted her berth to lay up redundant WW2 ships. In early December 1949, they had this distinguished hulk towed out to sea, to a point some nine miles south east of Selsey Bill, with orders that she be scuttled. A controlled charge of explosives was set by a naval party, with a loud muffled roar the old Trafalgar veteran simply settled down by one deck, still afloat in an upright postion, she had defied destruction. The decision was taken to radio Portsmouth and summon the powerful dockyard tug *Alligator*, this heavy workhorse was ordered to come out and ram the old wooden hulk. The tug duly arrived and after several powerful rushes, the *Implacable* turned over and slipped slowly beneath the waves. A Petty Officer from the Destroyer *Finisterre* who observed her final end, told me the crew around him fell silent as they witnessed her sinking.

The *Duguay Trouin* had been launched at Rochefort in 1797. After her capture in 1805, she was readily accepted into the Royal Navy and renamed *Implacable*. In 1808 under Captain Byam Martin, the *Implacable* captured the Russian war ship *Sevolod*, an action commemorated by the clasp to the NGS medal: **Implacable 26 Augt 1808**. In this battle she served under the direct orders of her old adversary *Victory*, now flying the flag of Admiral Sir James Saumarez.

The last major action of Implacable was in 1840, in this action her Captain, Edward Harvey, was awarded the St. Jean d'Acre medal in gold, together with a presentation sword from the Sultan of Turkey, these distinctions of gallantry were bestowed for the part played by *Implacable* during the capture of the fortress of Acre. This action was also commemorated by the clasp Syria to the NGS medal. Captain Harvey was awarded the Syria clasp to his NGS medal, it was to be his second clasp, the first being

The Royal Navy in December 1949, attempt to sink HMS Implacable, originally the French prize Duguay Trouin, the last surviving French man of war that fought at Trafalgar. At the moment of explosion this old fighting ship is flying the French Tricolor alongside the Royal Navy White Ensign. The charges laid by a naval party fail to do more than settle her down by one deck. Later a dockyard tug was to ram this historic ship, until finally she turned over and slipped slowly under.

Camperdown. A staggering 43 years battle service was to be shown between the two clasps on Harvey's NGS medal, - Camperdown 1797 and Syria 1840.

In 1855 *Implacable* became a Royal Navy training ship being moored off Torpoint, together with *Lion* they formed part of the Devonport training establishment. Until her untimely end in December 1949, she had spent 150 years afloat, more years afloat than *Victory*. Her sterling service in the Royal Navy had proved a good return indeed for the original prize money paid out after her capture in 1805.

Division of Monies

The total combined sum of Parliamentary grant and Naval prize money was to be divided according to rank, the prize money division followed precisely the rules as laid down in Admiralty regulations, The Parliamentary Grant was administered by trustees which included John Earl Spencer and Lord Howick. The total combined monies awarded being made up as follows:

Captains £3,362
Lieutenants, Masters and Captain of Marines £226
Pursers, Gunners, Surgeons, Master's Mates and Lieutenants of Marines £153
Midshipmen, Clerks, Gunner's Mates, Sergeants of Marines, Boatswain's Mates £37
Seamen and Marines £6-10-0d

Master's Mates had a pay rate in 1806 of between £2-12-6d to £3-16-6d per month, this according to the rated ship they served on. For a Master's Mate serving on *HMS Victory*, a 100 gun First Rate ship, the monetary reward for that day's work, amounted to more than three years normal pay. But that was nothing compared to a Captain of a First Rate ship, Thomas Masterman Hardy, as Captain of the *Victory* found his share of the Parliament grant coupled with the Naval prize money amounted to £3,362, which worked out at more than nine years pay. Whereas an Able Seaman serving on *Victory* who was paid £1-13-6d per month, received only £6-10-0d, amounting to less than four months regulation pay.

Traditionally the issue of prize money was in the first instance adjudicated by the High Court of Admiralty in London, also by Vice Admiralty Courts which existed in some British coastal ports and overseas possessions. Advertisements were placed, including in the London Gazette, confirming that prize money was ready to be paid against a named captured ship, ready for those involved to submit their claim, most naval officers had agents to claim the money for them. This system helped officers who were away at sea, and those who preferred to have dealings with the Admiralty Courts handled by a third party. Agents took a commission for this service.

So it was no wonder that in the aftermath of the battle and distribution of monies, a cartoon appeared by Tegg of Cheapside, playing on this very point. It showed a sailor on deck praying beside a cannon, the passing officers enquires, "Why sailor how is this at prayers when the enemy is bearing down upon us, are you afraid of them?" the sailor turns from his prayers and replies, "Afraid no! I was only praying that the enemies shot may be distributed in the same proportions as the prize money, the greatest part among the officers."

MONTHLY PAY FOR NAVAL OFFICERS AND MEN DURING THE TRAFALGAR PERIOD

The monthly wages shown against each rank and branch of service in the last column of the 'Rewards and Wages' table, relate to wages drawn by men of the Royal Navy and Royal Marines just after the Battle of Trafalgar. The table gives a good idea of rates of pay in 1806, this being about the same time as the bounty and prize monies were being calculated for the victorious sailors.

Men of the Royal Marines during this early part of the Napoleonic war were paid under two different systems. On land, marines received a higher rate of pay than serving afloat. A private of marines received £1 8s 0d per lunar month on land, this was reduced to 19s 3d per month as soon as he was mustered at sea. After seven years service he would be paid an additional 2s 4d monthly on land and 1s 9d whilst afloat, after fourteen years service this rate was increased to 4s 8d on land and 3s 6d at sea. The reason for differing rates of pay for land and sea service, was linked to victualling and accomodation costs. On land the marine would have to pay for his accomodation and victualling, but at sea his food and hammock was provided free.

The marine like the seaman had other charges levied against his pay. On board ship a percentage of his wages went to fund the chaplain and the surgeon's remunerations, a deduction of 6d a month was taken towards the running of the Greenwich Naval Hospital, and a further 1s per month was deducted for the "Chatham Chest," a fund for distressed seamen. Bedding and working clothes known as 'slops' had to be paid for, although the distinctive marine uniform worn on guard duties and during action was provided and paid for by the Admiralty.

After the mutiny of 1797, there followed many petitions from the lower deck to their senior officers, some making envious comparisons with the pay enjoyed by soldiers. The Lords of the Admiralty with the French war uppermost in their minds, introduced a monthly increase of 4s 6d for lower ranks and 5s 6d for petty officers. In 1806 after the victory of Trafalgar, a new improved pay structure was established. There existed a scale of pay for officers and men that was set against the rate of the ship in which they served, this scale of pay was directly linked to the number of guns carried by a Royal Navy ship. The pay for instance of the Master in a First Rate ship would be £12 12s 0d per month, Second Rate £11 11s 0d, Third Rate £10 10s 0d, Fourth Rate £9 9s 0d, Fifth Rate £8 8s 0d and Sixth Rate £7 7s 0d.

The only exceptions to this six stage scale of pay were to be Lieutenants, Chaplains, Sailmakers, Ropemakers, Caulkers and those whose monthly pay fell in the £1 13s 6d pay band or less.

At the top end of the pay scale was the full Admiral his basic pay was £3 1s 0d per day or £85 8s 0d per lunar month. In addition to this he received £1 10s 0d per day allowance to feed official guests on board.

Commanders-in-chief were allowed a secretary paid for by the Admiralty, in some cases at a rate of £150 or more per annum. The secretary would often have to pay towards the clerk who worked so closely with him. Mr Scott of the *Victory* acted as interpreter for Nelson and was considered his confidant. It is possible Nelson would have additionally funded his secretary.

CREW OF VICTORY AT TRAFALGAR, REWARDS AND WAGES

Rank	Prize Money	Government Grant	Monthly Pay
Captain Thomas Masterman Hardy	£973 0s 0d	£2,389 7s 6d	£32 4s 0d
Lieutenant of flagship	£65 11s 0d	£161 0s 0d	£9 2s 0d
Master	£65 11s 0d	£161 0s 0d	£12 12s 0d
Captain of Marines	£65 11s 0d	£161 0s 0d	£9 0s 0d
Carpenter	£44 4s 6d	£108 12s 0d	£5 16s 0d
Boatswain	£44 4s 6d	£108 12s 0d	£4 16s 0d
Gunner	£44 4s 6d	£108 12s 0d	£4 16s 0d
Purser	£44 4s 6d	£108 12s 0d	£4 16s 0d
Master's Mate	£44 4s 6d	£108 12s 0d	£3 16s 6d
Surgeon, William Beatty	£44 4s 6d	£108 12s 0d	£11 11s 0d
Lieutenant of Marines	£44 4s 6d	£108 12s 0d	£3 5s 0d
Chaplain to Lord Nelson	£44 4s 6d	£108 12s 0d	Admiral's discretion
Secretary to Lord Nelson	£44 4s 6d	£108 12s 0d	Admiral's discretion
Midshipman	£10 14s 0d	£26 6s 0d	£2 15s 6d
Clerk	£10 14s 0d	£26 6s 0d	£2 15s 6d
Armourer	£10 14s 0d	£26 6s 0d	£2 15s 6d
Surgeon's Mate/Assistant Surgeon	£10 14s 0d	£26 6s 0d	£2 15s 6d
Master at Arms	£10 14s 0d	£26 6s 0d	£2 15s 6d
Carpenter's Mate	£10 14s 0d	£26 6s 0d	£2 10s 6d
Caulker	£10 14s 0d	£26 6s 0d	£2 10s 6d
Ropemaker	£10 14s 0d	£26 6s 0d	£2 10s 6d
Sergeant of Marines	£10 14s 0d	£26 6s 0d	£2 5s 9d
Quartermaster	£10 14s 0d	£26 6s 0d	£2 5s 6d
Boatswain's Mate	£10 14s 0d	£26 6s 0d	£2 5s 6d
Sailmaker	£10 14s 0d	£26 6s 0d	£2 5s 6d
Gunner's Mate	£10 14s 0d	£26 6s 0d	£2 5s 6d
Yeoman of the Powder Room	£10 14s 0d	£26 6s 0d	£2 5s 6d
Armourer's Mate	£10 14s 0d	£26 6s 0d	£2 5s 6d
Ship's Corporal	£10 14s 0d	£26 6s 0d	£2 5s 6d
Caulker's Mate	£10 14s 0d	£26 6s 0d	£2 6s 6d
Coxswain	£10 14s 0d	£26 6s 0d	£2 2s 6d
Yeoman of the Sheets	£10 14s 0d	£26 6s 0d	£2 2s 6d
Quartermaster's Mate	£10 14s 0d	£26 6s 0d	£2 0s 6d
Sailmaker's Mate	£1 17s 6d	£4 12s 6d	£1 18s 6d
Captain of the Forecastle	£1 17s 6d	£4 12s 6d	£2 0s 6d
Captain of the Foretop	£1 17s 6d	£4 12s 6d	£2 0s 6d
Captain of the Maintop	£1 17s 6d	£4 12s 6d	£2 0s 6d
Captain of the Afterguard	£1 17s 6d	£4 12s 6d	£2 0s 6d
Captain of the Waist	£1 17s 6d	£4 12s 6d	£2 0s 6d
Trumpeter	£1 17s 6d	£4 12s 6d	£2 0s 6d
Sailmaker's Crew	£1 17s 6d	£4 12s 6d	£1 16s 6d
Quarter Gunner	£1 17s 6d	£4 12s 6d	£1 16s 6d
Carpenter's Crew	£1 17s 6d	£4 12s 6d	£1 16s 6d
Gunsmith	£1 17s 6d	£4 12s 6d	£1 15s 6d
Purser's Steward	£1 17s 6d	£4 12s 6d	£1 15s 6d
Cook	£1 17s 6d	£4 12s 6d	£1 15s 6d
Able Seaman	£1 17s 6d	£4 12s 6d	£1 13s 6d
Ordinary Seaman	£1 17s 6d	£4 12s 6d	£1 5s 6d
Corporal of Marines	£1 17s 6d	£4 12s 6d	£1 6s 6d
Drummer of Marines	£1 17s 6d	£4 12s 6d	£1 8s 5d
Private of Marines	£1 17s 6d	£4 12s 6d	£1 3s 9d
Landsman	£1 17s 6d	£4 12s 6d	£1 2s 6d
Boy 1st Class	£1 17s 6d	£4 12s 6d	£9 per annum
Boy 2nd Class	£1 17s 6d	£4 12s 6d	£8 per annum
Boy 3rd Class	£1 17s 6d	£4 12s 6d	£7 per annum

THE RANKS AND THEIR DUTIES ON BOARD VICTORY

Lieutenant. Being a 'Sea officer', a term which embraced lieutenants to admirals, Sea officers held a commision from the Admiralty, other officers such as masters and surgeons, held only warrants from the Navy Board. Lieutenants were trained in seamanship, navigation and gunnery, but would be expected to oversee and be familiar with all areas of the ship, including those of the carpenter, gunner and purser. A lieutenant if successful in actions against the enemy, could gain swift promotion.

Master. He was responsible under the Captain, for the sailing of the ship. All matters relating to navigation were his responsibility, in any part of the ocean he could determine longitude by his chronometer and latitude by his sextant, and know his vessel's whereabouts in daylight or darkness. His navigation calculations were recorded in the log-book. The master had the ability to make maps when neccessary.

Carpenter. Was responsible for the fabric of the ship, in storm or action he was the man for emergencies. He had a knowledge of shipbuilding and could organise the replacement or repair of damaged timbers. Carpenters would repair the damage done by the enemy, and if need be carry the ship into port under jury rig when her masts had gone. Other duties included checking the caulking of the seams, inspecting the spare yards and top masts, also seeing that the ship's boats were kept in good order.

Boatswain. His duty was to supervise the everyday work up aloft. It has been said he was resonsible for the actual motion of the ship, it was up to him to see that the rigging, sails, ropes, pulleys and blocks were all in good working order. Once the master advised the sailing instructions to the officer of the watch, these orders were passed to the boatswain who was responsible for the reefing and furling of sails. His whistle was his badge of authority, which he used to pipe all hands on deck.

Gunner. The gunner was responsible for the armament of the ship. On *Victory* he was responsible for more than a hundred tons weight of solid iron shot, they had to be stored so as to be kept free from rusting. The powder was kept in two felt lined magazines situated below the water-line, safe from enemy shot. For safety the magazines were covered by copper hatches. So important were these magazines that the keys were kept by the Captain. The armoury or gun room was the gunner's headquarters, this is where all the muskets, pistols, pikes, blunderbusses and cutlasses were kept. In action hundreds of crew members would man his guns.

Purser. An officer appointed by warrant to take charge of the provisions of the ship. To obtain his position he had to lodge a considerable sum of money as sureties. Under his immediate care were all the cotton, flannel and linen required for the clothing of the entire ship's company. The purser had charge of all the food, the beef, pork, butter, cheese, flour, sugar, treacle, cocoa and oatmeal. Also the wine, rum, brandy and grog. He was a wholesale tailor, provision and wine merchant, all rolled into one, in such a position a dishonest man could make a lot of money, hence the Admiralty insisted the purser deposit a large sum of money as security against fraud. Invariably pursers were men of some wealth.

Master's Mate. A position usually filled by a midshipman who was still awaiting to pass his examination or to receive his commission. He took responsibilty on watches by serving as the Lieutenant's deputy. There could be six master's mates on a first rate ship like *Victory*, the senior one was usually the head of the midshipmans berth.

Surgeon. Having learned his trade before he came on board, he probably passed his exam at Surgeon's Hall in London. The Royal Navy had just over 700 surgeons at the time of Trafalgar. The surgeon had charge of the sick and hurt on the ship and was expected to perform operations when required, especially amputations. All treatment given to the men was entered in a journal, which was examined at times by his superiors. On his recommendation, sick men could be transferred to shore hospitals or hospital ships. After 1805 surgeons received a sustantial increase to their pay.

Midshipman. Usually aged between fifteen and twenty-three. Midshipmen were training to be lieutenants, a first rate ship would have twenty four. Some continually failed their exams, and were still midshipmen at the age of 40 years plus! The young midshipmen during the celebrations on board *Victory*, amused all by their fun and joy.

Master at Arms. He held a warrant for his postion, which included teaching the men the use of muskets and small arms. It was his responsibility to see all fires and lights of the ship were out at the correct times, he kept a watch on the behaviour of the crew.

Sergeant of Marines. At Trafalgar there was only two non-commised ranks in the marines, corporals and sergeants. In action the sergeant commanded the musket firing of the marines. Unlike the marine corporals and privates who carried muskets, the sergeant carried a halberd or pike as his side arm. When the crew went ashore, a party of marines led by the sergeant would be present, to watch against desertion.

Quatermaster. Duties consisted of stowing the supplies, coiling cables on their platforms, and overlooking the delivery of provisions. Usually good mature men.

Boatswain's Mate. The sergeant major of the navy. He awoke the crew in the mornings for duty. With a loud voice he signalled the ship's commands. His rope end was the ship's 'starter', encouraging slow men. Floggings were administered by him.

Yeoman of Stores. Boatswains, carpenters and gunners all had large quantities of stores. Each store had a yeoman who took care of the contents. The most important store was that looked after by the yeoman of the powder room, this importance was reflected in his rate of pay, which was the same as the boatswain's mate.

Admiral's Retinue. The Admiral's own company of officers and servants, normally carried and paid for in addition to the normal compliment of the ship.

Supernumerary. A term to denote crew in excess of the ship's normal compliment. It was possible for men to be borne for wages in one ship and victuals in another. For obvious reasons he had to be victualled on the ship where he actually found himself. Sometimes the term 'Supernumary' was used for some of the Admiral's Retinue.

Gun Crews. Each 32-pounder gun needed seven men to man it, 18-pounders required six men. With the flag ship having 104 guns of various sizes, it took hundreds of men to fight a fleet action. When the firing was on one side of the ship only, crews would leave the idle side to help fire the guns on the action side. All men would be expected to man the guns, in the case of Joseph Burgin, ship's poulterer, he was in the thick of the action on the middle gun deck, having his leg smashed by enemy shot.

Able Seaman. A man who can work well, being aquainted with his duties as a sailor.

Ordinary Seaman. A man who is useful on board, but not an expert or skilled sailor.

Landsmen. Men without any sea experience, often pressed men from shore lives.

Boys. Were rated in three classes. Boys 3rd class, usually under fifteen years of age and were paid £7 per annum. Boys 2nd class, usually under eighteen years of age, these were paid £8 per annum. Boys 1st class would be training to become officers and were paid £9 per annum.

Marines. Acted as sea-going infantry, they also did guard duties on board ship, prime amongst these was the guarding of the Captain's cabin. Marines were also posted to guard the magazine and other store hatches including the spirit store. *Victory* had 145 Marines mustered at the time of the Battle of Trafalgar.

CLOTHING WORN BY VICTORY'S SAILORS DURING 1805

The rating on board *Victory* did not wear a standard uniform, they were allowed to dress generally as they liked, but in practice they followed and conformed to a style expected on a Man of War. A store of bedding and clothing was supplied by the Navy Board and held onboard by the purser, items could be sold to the crew by means of deductions from their wages, these necessities were known as 'Slops'. The purser's store of clothing contained no variety, it conformed to stock and standard patterns purchased in bulk by the Admiralty, thus issued clothing tended to be of a uniform nature and quality.

Men were dressed generally in the following mode. They often wore check shirts and white or buff trousers made of canvas, duck or jean type material. The trousers were short in the leg and loose at the ankle, coloured stockings and low cut shoes or pumps with neat buckles or large bows was common. Waistcoats were red of buff, sometimes with a flowered or stripe design, but it would seem red was the preferred colour. Over the waiscoat came a blue jacket cut very short in the waist, with two or three rows of buttons, the coat had no collar, but a handkerchief was worn round the neck and knotted. The favoured kerchief at this period was black silk, the object of this form of light scarf was to protect the tunic from the waxed pigtail. The pigtail which had become fashionable at the turn of the century, had by 1805 increased in size and weight, the sailor would add grease or wax, sometimes the wearer would even stiffen it by adding straw, all this to give the fashionable pigtail rigidity. Upon his head would be worn a woollen 'monmouth' cap, or a straw hat that was often enamelled black to make it waterproof, around the crown would be a ribbon tied with a large bow, on the ribbon the ships name *Victory* would be painted, or in some cases engraved on a small copper plate attached to the hat ribbon.

If a seamen died in service or from injuries sustained in action, his clothes were 'sold at the mast,' that is to say a form of auction took place, the money raised went for the benefit of his dependants, often his friends would pay extravagant prices for their comrade's clothes. The purser took charge of these 'dead mens clothes,' records of these transactions were kept in the ship's muster book. Listed under the name of the deceased were entered the details of each item of his clothing and the sum paid for them, the cost would be set against the name of the purchaser, it might well be the money bid for the clothes would be paid later from wages yet to be received.

Of the 57 men killed in action on *Victory* at Trafalgar, 41 of these 'discharged dead' sailors had their clothes sold in this manner to their shipmates. These accounts entered in the ship's Muster Table were considered so important that the itemised details and money obtained had to be confirmed as correct by the signatures of Captain Thomas Masterman Hardy, the Master Mr Thomas Atkinson and the Purser Walter Burke.

From these listed details of their sold clothes, it does help to build up a picture of how the sailor dressed in 1805, and how much clothing they carried aboard. Possessions were stowed in a chest or kept in a canvas sack hung from hooks below deck. Andrew Sack, Yeoman of sheets, 35 years of age, originally from Geneva, Switzerland, was one of those killed early in action on 21st October 1805. He was killed during the thick of the battle and had to be buried at sea quickly, (thrown overboard). This instant disposal of the body was neccessary to keep the decks clear of debris and gore during all the frantic activities that take place during a close fighting engagement. Andrew Sack had his effects listed in the muster book as being sold to eleven different seamen. It is quite surprising to find how much clothing was considered neccessary for one man to have with him on *Victory*, add to this listing the the full set of clothes he was wearing at the time of his burial at sea, and it becomes apparent he was well provided for against all circumstance of wear and foul weather. I have set out the details entered by the clerk, showing those named men who had made the purchases from the estate of Andrew Sack, and at what they paid the purser.

348 William Terrant: One Chest. 1/6d
713 Thomas Pickering: Jacket, waistcoat, 2 shirts and frock. £1.10s.0d
 89 Robert Shadd: Jacket, waistcoat, trousers and five shirts. £2.5s.0d
426 John Appleby: Three pairs of trousers, frock and shirt. £1.10s.0d
385 George Aunger: Three pairs of trousers, hankerchief, shirt, 2 pairs socks. £1.3s.0d
105 James McDonald: Two pairs of trousers, 3 frocks, 1 hankerchief. 18/-
412 George Prescott: One pair of boots. £1.2s.0d
262 William Welsh: Four pairs of stockings, hankerchief and shoes. £1.0s.0d
590 Thomas Dennison: 2 frocks, 1 waistcoat, 1 shoes. £1.5s.0d
191 John Thomas (1). One shirt, 1 shoes and 1 frock. £1.0s.0d
485 David Smith: 1 shoes and hankerchief. 10s. 6d

Interestingly the fashion items of hankerchiefs and waistcoats had ready buyers. Compare these prices against that required for new items from the purser's store, it shows that the men were most charitable with their bids for the clothes, they did what they could to assist the widow or relatives of their fallen shipmates.

The purser's store on *Victory* was fully stocked in March 1803, the date when the ship was ready for her active commission, after completing the three year refit in Chatham Dockyard. This store of clothing and bedding was intended to last for the duration of her service away from home waters, which in this case was to be well over two years. The individual items and their cost, as entered in the purser's account book, are shown below:

Mens clothing held in the purser's store:
Jackets 7s.2d. Shirts 4s.7d. Shoes 6s.0d. Stockings 2s.3d. Duck trousers 3s.0d. Duck frocks 4s.8d. Woollen trousers 4s.0d. Flannel jackets 3s.2d. Hats 3s.2d. Blankets 2s.7d. Beds 13s.0d or 16s.0d. each.

Boys clothing held in the purser's store:
Kersey jackets 4s.6d. Woollen trousers 2s.11d. Hats 2s.2d. Shoes 3s.5d. Duck trousers 2s.11d. Shirts 3s.3d. Duck frocks 3s.3d.

Although some seamen were lucky to have ample quantities of clothing like the late Andrew Sack, some others were less fortunate. 'Pressed' men taken off the streets of towns and ports, came with just the clothes they stood up in, these poor fellows needed a change of working clothes, especially in dirty weather. The purser's store was infact their salvation, even if it meant being in debt against future wages.

One recorded instance in April 1805, of an honest workman from Sheerness taken by the press gang of *HMS Revenge*, had unexpected results. William Collins was making his way home after a hard days work, he was working as a qualified stonemason on the building of the Sheerness defence works, a fortification needed against the possible invasion of Napoleon. The roving press gang from *Revenge* pounced and grabbed Collins, for all his protestations he was immediately taken out to the anchored *Revenge*, wearing only his light working clothes. Fortunately for him the incident was seen by a friend who quickly reported to the officer at the fortress, telling exactly what had happened to the stone mason.

William Collins was in the employ of His Majesty's Works at Sheerness, this building of the fortifications was under the command of Lieutenant Colonel Rudyord of the Royal Engineers. Collins was in fact in a 'reserved occupation', that is to say his importance to the defence of the realm, far outweighed the needs of any naval ship. A letter from Colonel Rudyord was quickly despatched to Captain Robert Moorsom of the *Revenge*. That letter is reproduced here:

CAPTAIN MOORSOM **Zealand at the Nore** 5th April 1805
OF HIS MAJESTY'S
SHIP REVENGE.

> It is my direction you discharge William Collins an impressed man from the
> Revenge who is employed in Our Majesty's Works at Sheerness, agreeable
> to Lieutenant Colonel Rudyord's request. *Signed B. Rowley, Ordnance Office.*

In this case the lucky man was returned to his important work on the fortification, by the intervention of the Lieutenant Colonel of Royal Engineers. Even so had the action to have him returned not been undertaken immediately, the ship would have sailed and poor William Collins may well have served on *Revenge* at Trafalgar, dressed as a stonemason.

Exemption certificates did exist to protect individuals against forcible inducement by the roving press gangs. These certificates were carried by Lighthouse keepers, who also wore badges proclaiming their protected status. Young men serving apprenticeships were protected, in the case of mercantile marine apprentices, they had protection for the first three years of their six year indenture. Press gangs were legal under British law, they were feared and hated by all, and particularly loathed by Masters of merchant ships, who suffered dreadfully from raids made on their ships and crews. It was easy to send a boarding party to merchant ships approaching or leaving ports, to obtain crews for Royal Navy ships. Men would put up stiff fights against the well armed press gangs. In 1794, the figate *Aurora* sent a press gang to board the merchant ship *Sara and Elizabeth* of Hull, the men resisted and during the scuffle the carpenter's mate was killed. A local coroner's jury found the Captain of *Aurora* guilty of murder. The Admiralty had him wisked away to the West Indies to escape justice.

The differing variety of clothing worn by the men shown in this engraving of the young Lieutenant Nelson, in the Lowestoffe's boat, November 1777, gives a good guide to the range of cothing worn on active service by seamen. The artist completed the work well after the event and the clothes are correct for 1805.

HISTORY OF LLOYD'S PATRIOTIC FUND
THE MONETARY AND GALLANTRY REWARDS

The Lloyd's Patriotic Fund was formed with the idea of raising suitable sums of money from commerce and the patriotic public, with the aim of rewarding army and naval gallant deeds. This recognition would be achieved by presenting gallantry rewards to officers, this was to take the form of decorated swords and silver vases. These presentation trophys were to be inscribed with the recipient's name and details of the heroic action for which he had been singled out for recognition.

The Patriotic Fund also distributed money for the wounded, this was bestowed to all who had suffered wounds in the service of Great Britain. The Fund would provide money for the widows and orphans of those men who perished in action.

The details of the rewards for gallantry and the recompenses for the wounded are fully described in the Lloyd's report published 1806, part of which is reproduced below, this deals specifically with the action of Trafalgar. The report reads:

It is resolved that vases to be presented to Nelson's family and to the Admirals associated with the victory, the value to be £500 and £300 each.

Captains and Commanders who survived the action would be presented with swords to the value of £100.

2nd class officers: Lieutenants and Captains of Marines, severely wounded £100, slightly wounded £50.

3rd class officers: Pursers, Gunners, Surgeons, Master's Mates, if severely wounded £50, slightly wounded £30.

4th class officers: Midshipmen, Clerks, Gunner's Mates, Sergeants of Marines, Boswain's Mates, if severely wounded £40, slightly wounded £25.

Seamen and Marines: Those severely wounded £20, for the slightly wounded £10.

Officers could be awarded additional gratuities if disabled in consequence of their wounds. Seamen and Marines disabled by their wounds to receive £40.

For those killed in action a sum would be made available to the relatives as soon as their situation was made known to the committee.

The Lloyd's Patriotic Fund Committee would meet when events and conflicts determined their attention to consider rewards. The Chairman would call for a meeting and the members would sit at a table to hear the engagement dispatches read out from the London Gazette. After consideration and deliberation by the committee, the Chairman would instruct the clerk to note the rewards decided on, the clerk would then mark against the names in the London Gazette what the Chairman had instructed. The Lloyd's Patriotic Fund Committee would come to a decision very soon after the publication of the battle report appeared in the London Gazette. For instance when the report of the engagement on 13 March 1806, of HMS *London* and *Amazon* with enemy ships, appeared in the London Gazette listing the wounded on May 6th, the Committee met seven days later on the 13th of May and detailed the monetary rewards to be paid to those men listed in the casualty report. In this case they exceeded their normal scale of payments and rewarded Lieutenant William Faddy of the *London* with £150 for his severe wounds and disablement. On another occasion a Lieutenant Edward Sibley of *Centaur*, wounded in action on 16 July 1806, received an enhanced sum of £200.

Edward Lloyd founded "Lloyds" business in a coffee house situated in Lombard Street, City of London in 1691. An early publication known as *Lloyd's News* was first published by him in 1696, later the title changed to *Lloyd's List* which then consisted entirely of shipping intelligence. As the business prospered greatly, a more impressive address was sought, so it was in 1774 that premises were acquired in the Royal Exchange, London. About this time a John Julius Angerstein who was born on the continent, became a member of the Committee of Lloyd's. His amazing business ability was recognised when in 1790 he became Chairman of Lloyd's, later he was Knighted for his services to the City. It was Sir John Angerstein with the support of Sir Francis Baring who initiated the establishment of large funds these were donated from a broad range of patriotic minded persons here and abroad, to support the victims of army and naval engagements during the French wars. The Lloyd's Patriotic Fund was founded on 20th July 1803, at a special meeting called at the Royal Exchange, London. Although a very generous gesture it was also a sensible and expedient move to protect the sea lanes and shipping business of Lloyd's.
The aims of this newly formed fund were described as:

"To animate the efforts of our defense by sea and land it is expedient to raise, by the patriotism of the community at large, a suitable fund for their comfort and relief, for the purpose of assuaging the anguish of their wounds or palliating, in some degree, the more weighty misfortune of the loss of limbs, or alleviating the distress of widows and orphans and granting pecuniary rewards or honorable badges of distinction for successful exertions of value or merit."

The mention of honorable badges of distinction refers to the presentation swords and the handsome silver presentation vases. The Patriotic Fund swords were awarded in three different values, £100, £50 and £30. The silver vases were likewise awarded in different values according to merit, the values being: £500, £300, £200 and £100. Lloyd's would bestow these swords and vases after the Patriotic Fund Committee had sat and considered the Admiralty report of the valiant action performed by the naval officer concerned.
The £100 sword was intended to be awarded to Captains and Commanders. As a rule the £50 sword were awarded to Naval Lieutenants and Marine officers, whereas the £30 sword would be awarded to Midshipmen or Mates. Only eighteen £30 swords were awarded. Although always referred to as a sword, the presentation piece was infact by its shape a sabre.

DESIGN OF THE SWORD

The presentation value of the sword was linked to the gallantry of the action and the status of the officer recipient. The amount of embellishment and craftsmanship entailed in making and assembling each grade of these swords, differed according to the award value. Lloyd's appointed Richard Teed, Sword Cutler of Lancaster Court, Strand, to craft and assemble these exceptional swords. Some of the components were made for Teed by outside craftsmen.
During 1803-1809, to pay a £100 for a sword was a outstandingly lavish sum, even so the work and finish on these presentation swords was of such a high standard it left little profit for the cutler.

The body of the scabbard was wood covered completely with gilt metal, attached to the £100 scabbard were two hangers in the form of serpents. The individual design of the £100, £50 and £30 value scabbards identify the type of sword it contained. The £100 sword is the most elaborate scabbard, with two cut out oval sections front and back covered in black velvet and overlaid with gilt heroic and classical designs, which include motifs of anchors, fasces, naval crowns, armour and sprays of laurel. Three further classical motifs appear overlaid on the main body of the gilt metal scabbard section, near the hilt is a cartouche showing a seated Britannia holding out the victor's laurel crown, towards the centre and at the point are cartouches showing the labours of Hercules. The £50 scabbard has the oval cut out panels scalloped along their edges but without embellishment over the shagreen, the scabbard hangers are two simple gilt rings. The £30 scabbard has three distinct separate gilt metal mounts affixed over the shagreen, the hangers are two gilt rings attached to gilt cabled retaining bands.

The design of every sword incorporated many details of heroic symbolism, a card provided with the cased award, gave the less informed young officer the description and key to what the embellishments signified.

In the late Georgian period the straight bladed sword was being replaced by the heavier broad curved sabre. The naval officer found these edged weapons more appropriate for the type of action he was likely to encounter, they were ideal to use when boarding enemy ships, or repelling borderers, their weight was often a decisive factor in the outcome.

The Patriotic Fund swords although designed in three different versions all shared the same type of classical hilt, these were of gilt metal, with the grips of diamond checkered ivory. The components of the hilt reflected the following human virtues. The knuckle-bar shaped as the club of Hercules with a snake entwined, this was to signify Herculean efforts combined with wisdom. The prominent Roman Fasces, which formed the quillons, signified National unity. The back strap formed in the likeness of the skin of Nemean lion, implied victory over great odds. A gold and blue bullion sword knot was entwined around the hilt. The blade of each sword was inscribed with the name of the recipient and the details of the action that gained the officer the reward. A typical £100 Trafalgar sword would have an inscription peculiar to the individual recipient. This was etched in three lines along the blade, which read:

FROM THE PATRIOTIC FUND AT LLOYDS TO ROBERT MOORSOM ESQ: CAPTN OF
H.M.S. REVENGE FOR HIS MERITORIOUS SERVICES IN CONTRIBUTING TO THE SIGNAL
VICTORY OBTAINED OVER THE COMBINED FLEETS OF FRANCE AND SPAIN OFF
CAPE TRAFALGAR ON THE 21st OCTOBER 1805.

Lloyd's Patriotic Fund presentation £100 swords for Trafalgar, of which there were twenty-three awarded, were slightly different from the traditional Lloyd's £100 sword, having in the design the recipient's initials etched within a multi-rayed star. The workmanship entailed in producing the magnificent gilt and blued effect on the blade will never be seen again, as the art of performing such beautiful work was never committed to paper and the craft was lost, it is known that mercury gilding was used applying the gold, a system that produces superb results but unfortunately is so deadly it eventually kills the craftsman with mercury vapour poisoning.

The Patriotic Fund foundation date of 1803 appeared on the sword's accompanying waist belt clasp. The year 1803 was a quiet period of the war with France, soon this was to change and the British Navy took the premier part in confrontation with the French. Many officers showed their mettle in some of the most spirited individual naval actions ever fought, their heroism richly deserved the rewards bestowed by the Patriotic Fund.

After approximately 150 swords and 60 silver trophys had been awarded during the momentous five years leading up to 1809, Lloyd's in May of 1809 decided to discontinue the presentations of the magnificently embellished swords, in future officers were to receive pecuniary rewards in lieu. This decision was prompted by the fact that Wellington's Peninsular Army, during the hard fought victories in Spain and Portugal, had suffered many casualties. Lloyd's Patriotic Fund committee decided they now needed to concentrate all their resources to relieving the hardships that resulted from these battles.

The presentations by the Patriotic Fund of silver vases, and on a few occasions silver tankards, to the value of £30, still continued, but from late 1809 the swords were no longer awarded under the Patriotic Fund.

Some officers who after this date had received Patriotic Fund monetary awards for their gallantry, would have much preferred the esteemed presentation swords, now discontinued. By this time the Lloyd's presentation edged weapons had become recognised by all serving officers as a gallantry decoration.

A few officers who had gained monetary rewards, approached the maker Richard Teed and asked to purchase a privately commissioned identical sword. He was only too ready to oblige, having been left with various parts of unassembled swords still in stock. With the Lloyd's contract terminated, Teed was not prepared to order further components from his outside suppliers. To be able to fulfill the gentleman's order, he found it expedient to use what he had available, which meant combining parts from £100, £50 and £30 swords to complete these private commissions. These later produced swords were assembled using parts from all three values, they are unkindly known today as "mongrels".

LLOYD'S PATRIOTIC FUND SILVER VASES

Officers who had been recognised for their gallantry, would in some instances be given the choice by the Patriotic Fund of either receiving a sword or an impressive silver presentation vase.

These silver vases were of the highest quality and superb examples of the silversmith's craft, they were designed by the artist John Flaxman, his artistic designs were crafted in silver by Benjamin Smith and Digby Scott of the Royal goldsmiths Rundell, Bridge and Rundell, a firm founded in 1790.

These silver vases like their associated swords came in various values, the main values bestowed upon officers would be the £50 vase and the £100 vase. For his gallantry and achievement at Trafalgar, Vice-Admiral Collingwood who took command of the victorious fleet after the death of Nelson, was awarded a vase to the value of £500.

The vase presented to the widow of Lord Nelson, Lady Viscountess Nelson was eventually the most expensive of all those presented by the Patriotic Fund, originally voted by the committee as a £500 presentation vase, with amendments to the original design to reflect the importance of this bestowal, the final sum actually paid by Lloyd's Patriotic Fund was £650.

A.   The Lloyd's Patriotic Fund £30 sword

The blade has the recipient's name and award details in small gold Roman letters on a stippled gilt background.
The scabbard body of wood is covered in polished shagreen encased with three separate gilt metal mounts, these sections are held in in place by ornate gilt cabled bands, from two of these bands the scabbard hanger rings are attached.

B.   The Lloyd's Patriotic Fund £50 sword

The blade has the recipient's name and award details in small gold Roman letters on a blue background.
The gilt covered scabbard is applied with relief cartouches, each depicting various Labours of Hercules, within naval trophy of arms. The scabbard has scalloped edges to the cut out oval sections, thus revealing the polished shagreen. The two scabbard hangers are in the form of gilt rings.

C.   The Lloyd's Patriotic Fund £100 sword

The blade has the recipient's name and award details in small gold Roman letters on a blue background.
The gilt covered scabbard is applied with relief cartouches, at the top a larger one showing Britannia holding a victors laurel, the others depicting various Labours of Hercules, all within naval trophy of arms. The oval cut out sections reveal black velvet, the velvet is heavily overlaid by a mass of intricate gilt heroic and classical motiffs. The suspender hangers are in the form of two gilt serpents.

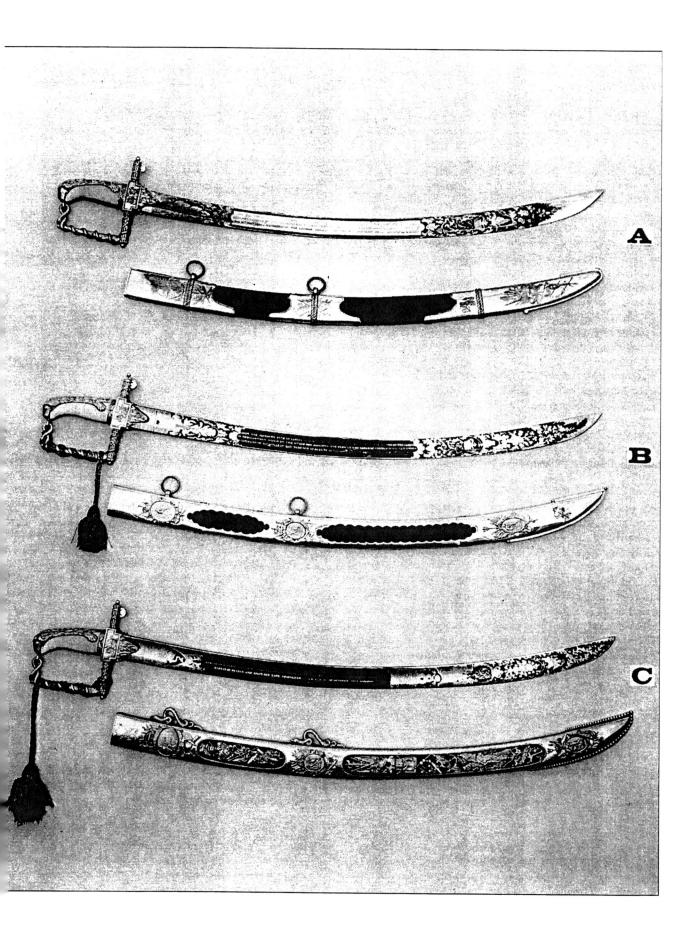

A

B

C

KEY TO THE FOLLOWING ROLL, FORMED FROM THE MUSTER TABLE OF HMS VICTORY

Column One: Name of officer or man as entered in the Muster Table. The surname appears first in capital letters followed by his forename, the spelling of the name is as interpreted by the clerk at the time of entry. Where abbreviations to the forename was written by the clerk as: '*Jos*' this might be for Joseph or Joshua, again '*Jno*' might indicate a John or Jonathan. If it was difficult to establish the correct first name, the clerk's abbreviation has been included.

Column Two: Gives the rank or trade of the man at the time of his appearance on *Victory*. As promotion and demotion could occur between the time of his appearance and October 1805, it was possible for a man to be advanced in rank or classification.

Column Three: Age of the officer or man at the time of his appearance onboard. There is always a chance for various reasons this may be incorrect. To arrive at the approximate age of the man at the battle of Trafalgar, refer to his age on appearance, see column five, and then calculate it on to October 1805.

Column Four: This shows his place of origin, sometimes entered as the village or town of his birth, or simply the country he came from. This information would be volunteered by the man to the clerk, who then made the appropriate entry.

Column Five: The date of appearance of the officer or man on *Victory*. In the case of a Royal Marine this column has been utilised to show the Division and Company the man was previously serving or training with. There existed at this time three Divisions: Chatham, Plymouth and Portsmouth. Each Division was allocated a series of Company numbers, which in the period up to 1814, were not duplicated in any other Division.

Column Six: Other related information. This will include such details as pressed men, casualties, medal entitlement and promotions for gallantry at Trafalgar. In a few cases the entry confirms the boy to have come from the Marine Society, this organisation took poor and destitute lads off the streets, gave them lodging and clothes, then trained them in marine matters which would assist them to gain entry to the Royal Navy. At one stage during the Napoleonic wars, the Marine Society provided five hundred lads a year to the navy.

Column Seven: Shows the muster number of the officer or man. A man would have only one muster number, this would be allotted on his appearance and would not change during the time he continually served on *Victory*, but if he was ordered away on duty elsewhere, his number would lapse, if by chance this same man returned to *Victory*, he may well be entered afresh on the 'Table' with a new muster number.

Muster prefix letter indicates:
M = Marine. B = Boy. S = Supernumerary. R = Admiral's Retinue.

ROLL OF MEN CONFIRMED AS SERVING ON HMS VICTORY FOR THE BATTLE OF TRAFALGAR. ADM 36-15900

Name as entered in Victory's Muster Table & alternative spellings	Rank or trade entered on Muster	Age on appearance	Home town or country	RM Div/Company and appearance date	Other related information and details	Muster number
ABBOTT John	Pte RM	20	Wellingborough	Chatham /91. 18/4/03		M78
ABRAHAMS William	AB	22	Amsterdam	11/5/03		326
ADAIR Charles William	Captain RM	27	Co Antrim, Ireland	Chatham/10. 14/4/03	Killed in Action	M1
ADAMS James	Quarter Master's Mate	26	Campbeltown, Argyll	21/5/03		628
ADAMS William	AB	28	Harwich, Essex	11/2/04	NGS Medal. Pressed Man	814
ALDCROFT Israel	ORD	26	London	10/9/05	Noted as Volunteer	964
ALDRIDGE James	AB	21	Heath, Hampshire	21/5/03		641
ALTOMARO Gaetano	Pte RM		Valletta, Malta	Chatham/100. 4/10/04		M178
ANDERSON Hans	AB	22	Norway	6/10/03	Wounded in Action. Volunteer	786
ANDERSON John (1)	AB	25	Exeter, Devon	11/5/03	NGS Medal	375
ANDERSON Thomas (1)	ORD	20	Dalkieth	11/5/03		M78
ANDREW George	Secretary's Clerk			29/3/05	Nelson's Retinue	R11
ANDREWS Isaac	LM	21	Clapham, London	11/5/03		145
ANNISON Josh	Supernumary			9/10/05		S923
ANSELE/ANSELL Thomas	AB	27	Barnett, Hereford	2/4/04		853
ANTONIE Antonia	ORD	23	St Nicholas, Wales	11/5/03		292
APPLEBY John	ORD	22	Yorkshire	11/5/03		426
ARCHIBALD James	ORD	39	London	14/6/03		720
ARTHUR John	LM	20	London	11/5/03		544
ASHTON William	Boy 3rd class	15	Manchester	13/10/05	Also listed as B3/45	S943
ASLETT Anthony	LM/ORD	20	London	11/5/03	NGS Medal	168
ASTIE Charles	AB	36	London	7/5/03	Noted as Volunteer	53
ATKINS William	LM	23	Charlestown, America	11/5/03		550
ATKINSON Thomas	Master	36	Halifax, Yorkshire	14/4/03	With Nelson at Copenhagen	31

Name	Rating	Age	Place	Date	Notes	No.
AUNGER George	ORD	21	Exeter, Devon	11/5/03	NGS Medal	385
BACON Richard	AB	45	Salisbury, Wiltshire	21/5/03		645
BAGLEY/BAGLAY James	Pte RM	18	Nottingham	Chatham/61. 17/4/03	NGS Medal	M67
BAGLEY Richard	Pte RM	19	Bilston, Staffs	Chatham/85. 14/4/03		M08
BAGLEY William	Pte RM	29	Stoke, Staffs	Chatham/7. 17/4/03		M59
BAILEY Thomas	Gunner's Mate	30	America	11/5/03	Took Nelson's last order to fire	588
BAKER Samuel	Pte RM	19	Dodford, Daventry	Chatham/43. 19/4/03		M139
BAPTISH John	AB	35	Rouen. Normandy	19/1/04		888
BARKAS Samuel	LM	21	Lancaster, Lancashire	11/5/03		185
BARLOW William	Pte RM	29	Crouth	Plymouth/18. 18/4/03		M98
BARNETT William	Gunsmith	29	Glasgow	11/5/03		224
BARRETT Josh	AB	22	Lisbon, Portugal	21/5/03		635
BARRETT Thomas	AB	35	Portsmouth, Hampshire	14/6/03		712
BARROW William	AB	25	Lewisham, London	11/5/03		353
BARRY John	ORD	40	Middleton	11/5/03		118
BARTLETT Thomas	AB	19	Martinstown, Dorset	31/7/03		921
BARTON Robert Cutts	Midshipman	18	Pembroke, Wales	31/7/03	Promoted to Lieutenant 1806	673
BATEMAN John	ORD	20	Windsor, Berkshire	9/3/05	NGS Medal	941
BEAGAN James	LM	24	Waterford, Ireland	11/5/03		199
BEATTY William	Surgeon	31	St Andrews, Scotland	31/12/04	Promoted Fleet Physician	908
BEAUMONT William	AB	20	Carlisle	11/5/03		419
BEETON/BEATON William	Pte RM	21	Sutton Montis, Somerset	Plymouth/18. 30/4/03		M150
BELL John	ORD	21	Gainsborough, Lincs	11/5/03		260
BELL William	ORD	18	Whitehaven	13/8/03	Noted as Volunteer	750
BENBOW Samuel	AB	45	London	11/5/03		435
BENJUA Josh	ORD	28	Malta	19/11/04		886
BENNETT Richard	Pte RM	30	Sedgley, Staffs	Chatham/13. 19/4/03	NGS Medal	M131
BENTOLE/BENTOTE James	LM	20	London	11/5/03	NGS Medal	113
BERRY James	Drummer RM	19	St John's, Norwich	Chatham/1. 14/4/03	Killed in Action	M5
BETSON/BEATSON Robert	AB	24	Fife, Scotland	26/9/05	NGS Medal	967
BIGGS William	Caulker's Mate	32	Somerset	11/5/03		175
BIRD Thomas	ORD	28	Pluntree, Notts	11/5/03		114
BIRD/BOYD Charles	AB	25	Liverpool	11/5/03	Detailed to Guns in action	345
BLACK Hugh G.W.	Boy 2nd class	14	Chatham, Kent	4/5/03	Noted as Volunteer	B2/3
BLAKE David	AB	20	Newcastle	11/5/03	Wounded in Action	399
BLIGH George M.	Lieutenant	19	Alverstoke, Hants	10/4/03	Wounded in Action. d 1834	19

Name	Rating	Age	Place of Birth	Date	Notes	No.
BLINKHORN Thomas	Pte RM	31	Isle of Ely	Chatham/99. 17/4/03		M41
BLUMBERRY Peter	AB	26	Gothenburg, Sweden	11/5/03		548
BOARD Phineas	Trumpeter	21	Newport	31/7/03		679
BOLL/BALL Henry	ORD	20	York	11/5/03	NGS Medal. Pressed Man	601
BOMKWORTH John	ORD	19	Smithfield	23/4/04	Wounded in Action	906
BOND William	AB	26	London	11/5/03	Wounded in Action	256
BOOKLESS Robert	Coxswain	27	Newcastle	11/5/03		393
BOOTH Thomas	LM	18	Saunton, Devon	18/8/03	Pressed Man	758
BOOTH William	LM	21	London	11/5/03		289
BORROW Patrick	Supernumary			9/10/05		S916
BORROW Philip	Supernumary	17		9/10/05		S924
BORTHWICK George	LM	20	Dalkeith, Scotland	11/5/03	NGS Medal	101
BOWE Patrick	AB	23	Wexford, Ireland	13/8/03		753
BOWEN Robert	AB	28	Dover, Kent	2/4/04		852
BOWER Valentine	Pte RM			Chatham/73. 28/6/04		M174
BOWLER John	LM	20	Deptford, London	11/5/03	Killed in Action	311
BOYES Charles	AB	24	Hanbledon, Hants	25/10/03		772
BOYLE Bernard	ORD	23	Donegal, Ireland	11/5/03		376
BRADFORD John	Pte RM	21	Broad Windsor, Dorset	Plymouth/48. 18/4/03		M119
BRADY William	ORD	36	Co. Cavan, Ireland	11/5/03		570
BRANNON Timothy	Quarter Gunner	27	Wicklow, Ireland	11/5/03		360
BRASBY/BRAZIL James	Quarter Gunner	36	Leinster, Ireland	11/5/03		215
BRASKETT John	AB	21	London	11/5/03	NGS Medal	183
BRENNAN John	Pte RM	42	Shannon, Ireland	Plymouth/15. 18/4/03	Killed in Action	M96
BRICE John	Pte RM	22		Plymouth/15. 18/4/03		M95
BROOKES John	Pte RM	28	Bristol	Chatham/4. 14/4/03		M17
BROWIS William	LM	18	North Shields	11/5/03		538
BROWN Jacob	Pte RM	19	Sudbury	Chatham/91. 18/4/03	NGS Medal	M80
BROWN John (1)	Pte RM	24	Cirencester, Gloucestershire	Plymouth/54. 18/4/03	Killed in Action	M112
BROWN John (1)	AB	23	Waterford, Ireland	11/5/03		178
BROWN John (3)	ORD	20	Amsterdam, Holland	11/5/03		327
BROWN John (2)	Pte RM	29	Stewarton, Ayrshire	Chatham/79. 18/4/03		M118
BROWN Jos. (Joseph)	ORD	25	London	11/5/03	NGS Medal	210
BROWN Joshua	ORD	30	Newbury, Berks	11/5/03	NGS Medal	176
BROWN Launcelot	Yeoman Powder Room	43	Sweednmouth	11/5/03	Wounded in Action	403
BROWN William (1)	AB	45	Mevagissey, Cornwall	11/5/03	Killed in Action	339

Name	Rating	Age	Birthplace	Date	Notes	No.
BROWN William (2)	ORD	25	Philadelphia, America	11/5/03	NGS Medal	473
BROWNE/BROWN George	Lieutenant of Signals	19	Bridgewater, Somerset	31/7/03	Noted as Volunteer	863
BROWNE James	ORD	21	Norwich, Norfolk	11/2/04		811
BROWNE John (5)	Gunner's Mate	30	Donegal, Ireland	21/5/03		643
BROWNING William D.	Pte RM	23	Malmsbury, Wiltshire	Plymouth/45. 18/4/03	NGS Medal	M125
BRYAN Thomas	ORD	21	Poole, Dorset	11/5/03		135
BUCHAN David	AB	23	London	11/5/03	Wounded in Action	330
BUCHAN James	Pte RM	19	Carlisle	Plymouth/39. 18/4/03		M107
BUCKLEY Cornelius	LM	29	Cork, Ireland	11/5/03	NGS Medal	468
BUCKLEY Thomas	Pte RM	27	Northwich, Cheshire	Chatham/61. 17/4/03		M69
BULKELEY Richard	Midshipman	16	America	31/7/03	Wounded in Action. Lt 1806	677
BULLOCK John	Pte RM	24	Tenbury	Chatham/98. 19/4/03		M143
BUNCE William	Carpenter	23		9/4/03		958
BURGESS James	Pte RM later Corporal	18	Chester	Portsmouth/32. 14/6/03	Wounded in Action	M165
BURGIN Joseph. Alias J. Coxhead	ORD. Poulter	30	Essex	11/5/03	NGS Medal. Wounded	269
BURKE Walter	Purser	65	Rochester, Kent	19/4/04	With Nelson when he died	802
BURLINGHAM John	LM	20	London	3/9/05	Noted as Volunteer	959
BURTON George	ORD	19	London	11/5/03	Wounded in Action	242
BUSH Frederick	ORD	22	Prussia	5/10/03	Pressed at Gibraltar	795
BUSH John	ORD	19	Norfolk	11/5/03	Wounded in Action	221
BUTCHER Henry	AB	24	Shields	11/5/03		314
BUTLER William	AB	20	Southwark, London	11/5/03	Wounded in Action	192
BUTTON Joseph (2)	LM	21	Chelmsford, Essex	11/5/03	NGS Medal	556
CAHARTY Patrick	AB	23	Donegal, Ireland	11/5/03		73
CALDWELL William	AB	29	Plymouth Dock, Devon	18/1/05		916
CALE William	LM	19	London	11/5/03		449
CALLAGHAN John	ORD	19	Bengal, India	11/5/03		308
CAMELANE Emanuel	ORD	24	Malta	19/1/04		887
CAMPBELL John (1)	LM	20	Netherlee	11/5/03		99
CAMPBELL John (3)	AB	20	Edinburgh	14/6/03		726
CAPELL Jacob	Pte RM	23	Queen Charlton, Somerset	Portsmouth/53. 14/6/03	NGS Medal	M153
CARR William	AB Supernumary	23	Gosport, Hampshire	10/9/05	Volunteer at Portsmouth	S5
CARRICK William	Pte RM	19		Plymouth/33. 17/4/03		M46
CARROLL Charles	Cook			9/4/03		6
CARROLL Cornelius	Boy 2nd class	11	Plymouth, Devon	4/5/03	NGS Medal. Volunteer	B2/2

Name	Rating	Birthplace	Age	Date	Notes	No.
CARRY Henry	ORD	Harwich, Essex	25	11/5/03		119
CARSLAKE William alias John	Midshipman	Colyton, Devon	18	18/4/03	NGS Medal. Lieut 22 Oct 1805	35
CARY Henry (2)	Midshipman	Portalington, Ireland	18	14/6/03	Master's Mate, Nov. 1805	687
CASEY Dennis	AB	Cork, Ireland	20	20/1/04		790
CASTLE William	AB	Newcastle	29	19/9/05	Wounded in Action	966
CASWELL John	ORD	Plymouth, Devon	20	2/4/04	Wounded in Action	838
CATON James	LM	Salvador, Brazil	26	11/5/03		249
CATTLING John	Boy 3rd class, Supn.	Harford, Devon	19	11/10/05	Also shown as Muster B3/40	S930
CAVANAGH Arthur	Boy 2nd class, Supn.	Belfast, Ireland	17	13/10/05	Noted as Volunteer	S942
CEPELL James	Armourer	London	34	27/8/04		867
CHAMBERS Thomas	Pte RM	Faversham, Kent	19	Chatham/1. 19/4/03	NGS Medal	M133
CHANT Isaac	AB	London	48	11/5/03		255
CHAPMAN James	LM	Edinburgh	20	11/5/03	NGS Medal	95
CHAPMAN James	ORD	Middlesex	20	2/4/05		945
CHAPPELL Charles	Pte RM	Thornbury, Gloucester	22	Chatham/43. 14/4/03	Wounded in Action	M24
CHAPPELL/CHAPELL Charles	Master's Mate, Supn.		21	9/10/05	NGS Medal. Wounded. d 1865	S928
CHASEMAN William	Master's Mate	Plymouth, Devon	21	17/4/03	Lieutenant 22 October 1805	34
CHEVALLIER H. Lewis	AB Retinue, Steward	Portsmouth volunteer		20/5/03	Nelson's Retinue	R3
CHIVERS John	Pte RM	Overton, Wiltshire	19	Portsmouth/142. 3/9/05		M181
CHRISTOPHER James	AB	Waterford, Ireland	23	3/8/04	Pressed Man at Oporto	898
CHURCH John	Pte RM	Yarmouth, Norfolk	26	Plymouth/15. 18/4/03		M97
CLARKE George	ORD	Stockport, Cheshire	23	11/2/04	NGS Medal. Volunteer	893
CLARKE Henry (1)	AB	Dublin	33	11/5/03		442
CLARKE Henry (2)	LM	Deptford, London	18	11/5/03		683
CLARKE James	AB	Chatham, Kent	32	21/5/03		639
CLARKE Samuel	ORD	Portesham, Dorset	20	11/2/04	Noted as Volunteer	816
CLARKE William	AB	Bedford	29	21/5/03	NGS Medal	660
CLAY John	Boy 1/Volunteer	Epsom, Surrey	18	3/8/04	NGS Medal	B1/20
CLEMENTS Michael	Ships Corporal	Canterbury, Kent	29	11/5/03	NGS Medal	355
CLOUGHTON Robert	Pte RM	Durham	36	Portsmouth/8. 14/9/05		M182
COATES Joseph	LM	London	22	11/5/03		429
COBOURNE/COWBOURN William	Pte RM	Bolton, Lancashire	33	Chatham/99. 17/4/03	Killed in Action	M42
COCKRAN George	Corporal RM	Greenock, Scotland	20	Plymouth/45. 18/4/03	Killed in Action	M85
COGSWELL William	Corporal RM	Wiltshire	20	Chatham/91. 14/4/03		M4
COLE Nathanel	AB	Sunderland	20	11/5/03		501
COLEMAN Benjamin	ORD	Dublin	27	14/6/03		729

Name	Rating	Birthplace	Age	Date	Notes	No.
COLLARD Thomas	AB	Hoffam, Lincolnshire	22	21/5/03	Wounded in Action	659
COLLINGWOOD Edward Francis	AB/Midshipman	Milford, South Wales	21	14/9/05	Lieutenant 1806	S9
COLLINS John (2)	Carpenter's Crew	Axminster, Devon	52	18/6/04		857
COLLINS Richard	AB	Philadelphia, America	21	11/5/03		151
COLLIVER Richard	LM	Oxfordshire	20	11/5/03		159
CONN David	LM	Stratford, London	22	10/5/03	Wounded in Action. Volunteer	61
CONNELL Joseph	ORD	Cuckolds Row, Scotland	25	11/5/03	NGS Medal	104
CONNOLLY Thomas	ORD	Galway, Ireland	32	11/5/03		465
CONNOR James	ORD	London	21	11/5/03		148
COOKE Benjamin	Pte RM		28	Plymouth/48. 18/4/03	Died of Wounds	M88
COOKE William (1)	Pte RM	Dublin	32	Chatham/91. 18/4/03		M106
COOKE William (2)	Pte RM	Sussex	37	Portsmouth/92. 14/6/03		M160
COOPER John	LM	Wandsworth, London	21	11/5/03		130
COOPER Samuel	AB	Bury, Lancashire	34	14/6/03	Wounded in Action	714
COPE John	AB	Bristol	22	11/5/03		77
CORMICK John	Boatswain's Mate	Wexford, Ireland	24	11/5/03		573
CORNWALL Thomas	ORD	Whithane	20	11/5/03		196
CORTEN George	LM	Oxford	30	11/5/03		112
CORWARDER John	ORD	London	21	11/5/03	Killed in Action	572
COSGROVE James	Purser's Steward	Dublin	40	8/9/04		878
COULSTON/COLSTONE George	Pte RM	Newcastle	21	Plymouth/143. 14/4/03	Wounded in Action	M12
COWLING William	Corporal to Pte RM	Peterborough	21	Chatham/46. 17/4/03	Denoted on 14 October 1805	M40
COWNLEY Thomas	Pte RM	Bewdley, Worcestershire	19	Chatham/49. 17/4/03		M37
CRAMWELL Henry	LM	Crayford, Kent	20	11/5/03	Killed in Action	263
CRAWLEY Timothy	ORD	Kinsale, Cork, Ireland	30	11/5/03	Noted as Volunteer	743
CROFTON Thomas	Pte RM	Dublin	25	Chatham/10. 14/1/03	Wounded in Action	M19
CROFTS Richard	Pte RM	Coventry	22	Plymouth/42. 18/4/03		M84
CROOKE Matthew	AB	Hornsey, Yorkshire	38	2/4/05		951
CRUIZE Thomas	ORD	Gosport, Hampshire	25	11/5/03		266
CUMMINS William	Pte RM	Campbeltown, Scotland	21	Plymouth/36. 18/4/03		M108
CURRAN John	ORD	Co. Carlow, Ireland	32	14/6/03		733
CURRY James	AB	London	24	11/5/03	Wounded in Action	343
DANIELS Thomas	LM	London	20	11/5/03	Killed in Action	125
DARBY George	ORD	Newcastle	21	11/5/03		162
DARBY Robert	AB	Darlington	23	11/5/03		342

Name	Rating	Age	Place	Date	Number	Notes
DARNOLD William	ORD	32	Herefordshire	11/5/03	425	Wounded in Action
DAVIS Charles (1)	ORD	36	London	11/5/03	295	Killed in Action
DAVIS Charles (2)	AB	24	New York, America	11/5/03	304	
DAVIS John (1)	ORD	24	Swansea, Wales	11/5/03	170	Pressed Man
DAVISON James	ORD	20	Aberdeen	11/5/03	609	Killed in Action
DAVISON/DAVIDSON Robert	AB	23	Sunderland	11/5/03	520	Wounded in Action
DEAN Nicholas	Pte RM	22	Honiton, Devon	Plymouth/42. 18/4/03	M86	Nelson's Retinue
DEAR Thomas	AB Retinue			10/9/05	R17	
DENNISON Thomas	AB	34	Co. Sligo, Ireland	11/5/03	590	
DICKSON John	LM	31	Norfolk	11/5/03	428	Wounded in Action. Gibraltar
DINTON James	ORD	22	London	11/5/03	74	
DIXON Christopher	Quarter Master	27	South Shields	11/5/03	398	
DIXON Thomas	LM	20	Edinburgh	11/5/03	100	
DIZMONT Daniel	ORD	33	Hairstown, Co Cork, Ireland	13/2/04	831	
DOAK William	Boy 1st class	18	Edinburgh	23/4/04	B1/27	Noted as a Volunteer
DOBBIN Peter	Qtr Master's Mte/AB	33	London	21/5/03	627	
DOBSON Isaac	Carpenter's Crew	25	Whitby, Yorkshire	18/8/03	760	Noted as Volunteer
DONNELLY Charles	AB	48	Liverpool	11/5/03	115	
DOUBLE/DOBLE Robert	Carpenter's Crew	22	St Ives, Cornwall	3/1/05	910	NGS Medal
DOWDEN Samuel	Sergeant RM	30	Co Monaghan, Ireland	Chatham/58. 14/4/03	M3	
DOWDING Thomas	Quarter Gunner	36	Dorset	11/5/03	458	
DOWNES William	Pte RM	32	Holbeach, Lincs	Chatham/76 . 17/4/03	M58	
DOWNES William	ORD	22	London	11/5/03	453	
DRAKE Samuel	ORD	30	Essex	11/5/03	226	
DRUCE Edward	ORD	26	Witney, Oxfordshire	2/4/05	950	Wounded in Action
DRUMMOND Robert	AB Retinue			31/7/03	R9	NGS Medal. Nelson's Retinue
DUBINE Dominick	ORD	28	Italy	11/5/03	559	
DUFFY Sam	ORD	26	London	11/5/03	293	
DUNKIN John	ORD	23	Co. Mayo, Ireland	11/5/03	576	
DUNN John	Pte RM	31	Calder	Plymouth/81. 18/4/03	M94	
DUPUIS John	ORD	30	Nantes, France	18/8/03	759	Noted as Volunteer
DUTTON John	Pte RM	24	Cheadle, Staffs	Plymouth/42. 18/4/03	M81	Wounded in Action
EAVES Francis	Yeoman of Sheets	28	Bristol, Somerset	4/5/04	856	NGS Medal
EBBS John	Gunner's Mate	26	Poole, Dorset	11/5/03	347	
EBBSWORTH John	Pte RM	36	Ashbury, Berkshire	Chatham/7. 14/4/03	M15	Killed in Action

Name	Rating	Age	Place	Date	Notes	Number
EDMUND/HENMAN John	ORD	27	London	11/5/03	Noted as Volunteer	66
ELLIOTT William	Master at Arms	31	Birmingham	22/4/03		40
EVANS James	ORD	27	Gloucester	11/5/03		184
EVISON Thomas	AB	24	Grimsby, Lincolnshire	13/8/03	Noted as Volunteer	745
FAIRMAN John	ORD	21	Beddington, Surrey	6/10/03	Noted as Volunteer	788
FALL William	AB	30	Dartford, Kent	14/6/03	Wounded in Action	732
FARECLOTH Robert	AB	22	Norfolk	9/3/05		937
FEAGAN James	Pte RM	31	Dublin	Chatham/43. 17/4/03	Wounded in Action	M36
FEARALL Daniel	Sergeant RM	27	Lewes, Sussex	Chatham/19. 19/4/03	NGS Medal	M129
FELTON John	Midshipman	21	Hackney, London	10/9/05	NGS Medal. Lieutenant 1806	962
FENNELL James	AB	25	Deptford, London	11/5/03		341
FENWICK George	Gunner's Mate	32	Newcastle	11/5/03		397
FERRENS William	AB	36	Dublin	2/4/04		836
FERRIS William	Boy 1st class	15	Ashbarton, Devon	1/8/03	Noted as a Volunteer	B1/14
FINLAY Robert	AB	32	Dundee, Scotland	18/1/05		917
FISSER John	AB	28	Norway	6/10/03	Noted as Volunteer	804
FITZGERALD John	ORD	24	Liverpool	11/5/03		554
FLEMMING William	AB	28	Yarmouth, Norfolk	11/5/03		220
FLIGHT Henry	Carpenter's Crew	44	Portsmouth	9/4/05		936
FLYNN Bernard	ORD	29	Rosconnon, Ireland	11/5/03		431
FLYNN Edward	Pte RM	30	Westminster, London	Chatham/58. 23/4/03		M148
FLYNN Matthew	LM	20	Dublin	11/5/03		160
FOLEY Stephen	ORD	39	Kinsale, Ireland	27/1/04		889
FOLEY Thomas	ORD	45	Tipperary, Ireland	5/10/03	Pressed Man at Lisbon	794
FORBES William	AB	42	North Shields	11/5/03		366
FORD Henry	Quarter Master	45	North Britain	21/5/03		657
FORD Richard	Agent Victualler, Supn			14/9/05	From Portsmouth	S906
FORD William	ORD	22	Charlton, Sussex	11/5/03		201
FORD William	Pte RM	22	Bristol	Chatham/58. 18/4/03		M75
FRANCOIS John	ORD	30	Curacoa, West Indies	18/8/03	Wounded in Action. Volunteer	695
FRENCH Francis	AB	27	Lynn, Norfolk	21/5/03	Pressed Man	632
FRENCH George	ORD	25	Stratford	11/5/03	NGS Medal	254
FRENCH James	AB	20	Harwich, Essex	11/5/03	Acted as gun loader in action	329
GALLAGHAN Edward	LM	25	Co. Mayo, Ireland	11/5/03		580

Name	Rank	Age	Place	Date	Notes	Number
GANTLETT John	AB	24	Southampton	11/2/04	Pressed Man	819
GARRICK James	AB	26	Shetland	11/5/03		124
GASBY Samuel	LM	20	Manchester	11/5/03		436
GENTILE Donque	Pte RM		Valletta, Malta	Chatham/100. 21/2/05		M179
GEOGHEGAN John	Agent Victuallers Clerk			8/10/05	Wounded in Action	S911
GIBBONS William	LM	28	London	11/5/03		500
GIBSON Robert	AB	25	Lynn, Norfolk	11/5/03	Wounded in Action	154
GIDDICE Joseph	ORD	19	Mere, Wiltshire	23/4/04		975
GILL James	AB	40	Poole, Dorset	21/5/03		637
GILLETT William	ORD	22	Dover, Kent	11/5/03	Wounded in Action	420
GILLMAN John	Sergeant RM	25	Cork, Ireland	Chatham/28. 17/04/03		M32
GING Michael	ORD	21	Belfast	20/1/04		969
GOBLE Thomas	AB/Master's Mate	23	Arundel, Sussex	5/10/05	NGS Medal. Secretary to Capt.	978
GODBY Philip	AB	43	Cricklade, Wiltshire	9 March 1805	Wounded in Action	939
GOODCHILD Thomas	ORD	20	Baldock, Herts	11/5/03		433
GORDON Joseph	ORD	21	London	3/8/04		973
GRAHAM John	AB	31	North America, Canada	6/10/03	Noted as Volunteer	787
GRAHAM Thomas	ORD	18	Margate, Kent	2/4/05	Wounded in Action	970
GRAHAM Thomas	LM	22	London	11/5/03	NGS Medal	261
GRAVES George	Pte RM	19	Oaknutt, Nottingham	Chatham/46. 18/4/03	Wounded in Action	M77
GREEN James	Mid/Master's Mate	22	Attlebridge, Norfolk	3/4/05	Lieutenant 1806	931
GREEN James	Pte RM	25	Lutterworth, Leicestershire	Chatham/4. 17/4/03	Killed in Action	M51
GREEN James	Quarter Gunner	41	Edinburgh	21/5/03		653
GREEN Samuel	Pte RM	23	Bilston, Staffs	Chatham/73. 19/4/03	NGS Medal. Wounded	M135
GREEN Thomas (1)	AB	28	Cork, Ireland	21/5/03	Wounded in Action	652
GREEN Thomas (2)	ORD	20	Hull, Yorkshire	13/8/03		754
GREENFIELD George	ORD	20	Dunbar, Scotland	3/8/04		976
GREGORY John	Pte RM	21	Potters Bar, Hertfordshire	Chatham/34. 17/4/03		M50
GREY Edward	ORD	20	Weymouth, Dorset	11/5/03	Wounded in Action	486
GREY John	AB	21	Falmouth, Cornwall	11/5/03	Wounded in Action	207
GRIFFEN/GRIFFIN William	ORD	28	Winchester, Hampshire	11/5/03		277
GRIFFITHS Griffith	AB	20	Carnavon, Wales	11/2/04	Noted as Volunteer	821
GRIFFITHS Michael	AB	22	Waterford, Ireland	2/4/04		843
GRIFFITHS William	Boy 3rd class	17	London	3/8/04		B3/34
GRINDALL Festing H.	Midshipman	17	Weymouth, Dorset	31/7/03	Son of Capt. Richard Grindall	678
GUINTI Giovanni	Pte RM		Messina, Sicily	Chatham/16. 17/5/04	Wounded in Action	M170

Name	Rank	Age	Place	Date	Notes	No.
GUTLIPSTER John	ORD	23	Denmark	11/2/04	Noted as Volunteer	854
HAGGERTY Thomas	AB	20	Newcastle	11/5/03	Wounded in Action	334
HALL John	ORD	22	London	11/5/03		444
HALL Peter	LM	20	London	7/5/03	Wounded in Action. Pressed	52
HALL William	AB	19	Newcastle	11/5/03	NGS Medal. Wounded	460
HALLETT William	ORD	18	London	11/5/03		408
HAMMOND Charles	Boy 3rd class			13/10/05		S945
HAMPTON Samuel	ORD	20	Godalming, Surrey	11/5/03		380
HANBURY William	Pte RM	29	Stapleford, Nottinghamshire	Chatham/76. 18/4/03	Wounded in Action. Volunteer	M76
HANNAM William	ORD	20	Calne, Wiltshire	11/2/04		808
HARDING Henry	Pte RM	30	Tring, Hertfordshire	Chatham/85. 17/4/03	NGS Medal	M47
HARDING Robert	Pte RM	19	Higham, Kent	Chatham/61. 17/4/03		M64
HARDY Jonathan	ORD	25	Grenada, West Indies	2/4/05		947
HARDY Thomas Masterman	Captain	36	Portisham, Dorset	31/7/03	Naval Small Gold Medal	665
HARRINGTON Daniel	Midshipman	29	Waterford, Ireland	3/8/05	Lieutenant Dec 1805	955
HARRIS George	AB	29	Halifax, Yorkshire	11/5/03	Wounded in Action	177
HARRIS Isaac	Pte RM	21	Denington	Plymouth/78. 18/4/03	Wounded in Action	M117
HARRISON William	ORD	26	Derby	21/5/03	NGS Medal	642
HARTLEY Matthew	AB	49	Kendal, Westmoreland	11/5/03		537
HARTNELL James	Ropemaker	27	Devonshire	11/5/03	NGS Medal	303
HARVEY William	AB	28	America	11/2/04	Noted as Volunteer	817
HAWKINS Benjamin	AB	26	London	11/5/03		117
HAWKINS Thomas	Pte RM	21	Ashbrittle, Somerset	Plymouth/27. 18/4/03		M121
HAYES James	ORD	19	Plymouth, Devon	11/5/03		163
HAYLE John	Pte RM	32	Woodbridge, Suffolk	Chatham/4. 14/4/03		M16
HEATH Isaac	Pte RM	22	Uphill, Somerset	Plymouth/105. 14/9/05		M185
HEATH John	Carpenter's Crew	23	Reading, Berkshire	11/5/03	NGS Medal	356
HEAVER Richard	ORD	25	Weymouth, Dorset	2/4/04		894
HENLEY Daniel	Ship's Corporal	35	Newbury, Berkshire	14/6/03		727
HENRIX Thomas	Pte RM	27	Canterbury	Chatham/85. 17/04/03		M44
HERWIN Arthur	ORD	20	Shetland	2/4/04	Killed in Action	845
HIGHLAND John	LM	22	Leeds, Kent	11/5/03	Noted as Volunteer	65
HILLIER Daniel	Pte RM	23	Uley, Gloucestershire	Plymouth/54. 18/04/03	Killed in Action	M114
HILLS Alexander	Lieutenant	25	Bedhampton, Hampshire	19/1/05	Informed fleet of Nelson's hurt	918
HINES James	Pte RM	21	Dorset	Plymouth/72. 18/4/03	NGS Medal. Wounded	M120

Name	Rating	Age	Place	Date	Notes	Number
HODGES George	Pte RM	24	Bristol	Chatham/40. 17/4/03		M39
HODGKINS Joseph	ORD	22	Battlebridge	11/5/03	Noted as Volunteer	280
HOFFMAN Peter	ORD	34	Holland	11/5/03	Wounded in Action. Pressed	70
HONNOR William	Quarter Gunner	20	London	9/5/03		59
HOWARD John	ORD	21	Co. Mayo, Ireland	11/5/03		577
HUBERT Aaron	Boy 2nd class	14	Cosham, Bristol	14/6/03		B2/20
HUGHSON Lawrence	ORD	20	Shetland	11/5/03		522
HULBERT James	LM	22	Wandsworth, London	11/5/03		107
HUMPHRIES William	LM	19	Carnarvon, Wales	5/10/03	Pressed Man at Lisbon	783
HUNNIFORD John	Boatswain's Mate	26	Dartmouth, Devon	13/8/03		751
HUNS John	Boy 3rd class	15	London	27/4/03	From the Marine Society	B3/3
HUNTER John	AB	21	Newcastle	11/5/03	NGS Medal	447
HUTCHINSON William	Boy 3rd class	13	London	23/4/04		B3/33
INWOOD William	AB	27	New York, America	14/6/03		730
IRELAND George	AB	53	North Shields	2/4/05		948
IVEY William	Corporal RM	22	Ilchester, Somerset	Plymouth/30. 18/4/03		M101
JACKSON John	AB	27	Philadelphia, America	2/4/04		850
JACKSON John	Pte RM	23	Northants	Chatham/82. 17/4/03		M38
JACKSON William	ORD	26	Edinburgh	11/5/03		94
JACOBS John	ORD	25	Arundel, Sussex	11/5/03		140
JAGO Thomas	LM	25	London	11/5/03		234
JAMESON Samuel	ORD	19	Lynn, Norfolk	11/5/03		439
JARVIS Thomas	AB	41	Whitby, Yorkshire	11/5/03		616
JATER Mark	ORD	18	London	3/8/04		974
JEFFERSON John	ORD	20	Finsbury Square, London	11/5/03	Pressed Man	233
JENNINGS Henry	Pte RM	23	Wolverhampton	Plymouth/45. 18/4/03	NGS Medal	M83
JEWELL Richard	ORD	22	London	11/5/03		251
JEWER Andrew	AB	23	Fife, Scotland	18/8/03	Killed in Action	757
JOHNS Thomas	AB	26	Carmarthen, Wales	11/5/03		271
JOHNSON Ezekiel	ORD	21	Kilbarchan, Scotland	3/8/04	NGS Medal	901
JOHNSON James (1)	Quarter Master's Mate	22	Newry	11/5/03		322
JOHNSON John	ORD	22	Newport, Rhode Island	11/5/03	NGS Medal	110
JOHNSON Samuel	AB	34	Blandford, Dorset	2/4/04		835
JOHNSON Thomas	Boy 3rd class	18	Naples, Italy	27/1/04	Noted as Volunteer	B3/38

Name	Rank	Age	Place	Date	Notes	No.
JOHNSON Thomas	Quarter Master	21	Southampton	21/5/03	Killed in Action	640
JOHNSON William	Boy 2nd. Supernumary	18	Manchester	11/10/05	Noted as Volunteer	S929
JOHNSON William	ORD	18	Liverpool	13/8/03		748
JOHNSTON William (2)	AB	33	Cheshire	9/3/05	Noted as Volunteer	938
JONES James	AB	28	Salisbury, Wiltshire	13/8/03	Pressed Man	741
JONES Morgan	AB	22	Carnarvon, Wales	11/2/04		823
JONES Peter	AB	29	Philadelphia, America	2/4/04		841
JONES William	Pte RM	26	Chepstow, Wales	Plymouth/69. 18/4/03	Killed in Action	M115
JONES William (1)	ORD	26	Hornchurch, Essex	11/5/03	Noted as Volunteer	365
JONES William (2)	AB	28	Angelsey, Wales	11/2/04		826
JONES William (3)	LM	24	Ruthin, Wales	11/2/04	Wounded in Action. Pressed	829
KELLY Peter	AB	24	Dublin	2/4/04		844
KENNEDY Archibald	AB	37	Greenock, Scotland	2/4/05		949
KENNEDY George	Pte RM	29	Rougham, Norfolk	Chatham/22. 17/4/03	Killed in Action	M53
KENNEDY John (2)	ORD	24	Dublin	9/7/03		736
KENNENSAW Stephen	ORD	22	Plymouth, Devon	13/8/03	Noted as Volunteer	742
KENNY Stephen	AB	29	Co. Carlow, Ireland	11/5/03		331
KENTALL John	ORD	20	Lambeth, London	11/5/03	Wounded in Action	283
KIDD John	Carpenter's Mate	25	Argylshire, Scotland	11/5/03		589
KILLEN Peter	ORD	20	Co. Louth, Ireland	11/2/04		828
KING Andrew	Lieutenant	25	Southampton	15/4/03	Commander 1806	27
KING John	Quarter Mstr/Yeo Sigs	54	Sunderland	11/5/03	Killed in Action	508
KING Thomas	Quarter Master's Mate	30	Yarmouth, Norfolk	11/5/03		179
KING William	ORD	18	Baltimore, America	11/5/03		302
KNIGHT William	Pte RM	22	Whitchurch, Hampshire	Plymouth/75. 18/4/03	Died of Wounds	M116
LAMBKIN William	LM	28	Horsmonden, Kent	9/5/03	Pressed Man	55
LANCASTER Henry	Boy 1st class	14	Wimbledon, Surrey	14/9/05	NGS Medal. Mid. Jan. 1806	B1/24
LANE George	Carpenter's Crew	24	London	9 March 1805		942
LANGSHAW John	ORD	20	Liverpool	11/2/04	Noted as Volunteer	892
LAUNDRY Thomas	AB	23	London	11/5/03		187
LAVENNY James	ORD	18	Dundee, Scotland	11/5/03		258
LAWRIE/LAURIE Thomas	ORD	20	Edinburgh	11/5/03	NGS Medal	253
LAY James	LM	22	Peckham, London	11/5/03		312
LAYKING/LAKING Charles	ORD	25	Cornwall	11/5/03	NGS Medal	578

Name	Rank	Age	Origin	Date	Notes	No.
LE COUTEUR/COUTH Nicholas	AB. Supernumary	20	Jersey	11/5/03	Wounded in Action	S936
LE DAM Hans	ORD	20	Denmark	3/8/04		899
LEACH William	Pte RM	25	Pettistree, Suffolk	Chatham/7. 17/4/03		M54
LEAKY John	Carpenter's Mate	38	Stonehouse, Devon	14/6/03	Wounded in Action	718
LEARY Daniel	AB	22	Cork, Ireland	11/5/03		275
LEARY James	ORD	22	Wexford, Ireland	14/6/03		709
LEEDS Thomas	ORD	20	Co. Down, Ireland	11/5/03		87
LEEK William	AB	39	Canterbury, Kent	11/5/03		142
LEGG Charles	LM	18	Deptford, London	11/5/03	Wounded in Action	243
LEGG Peter	ORD	21	Waterford, Ireland	2/4/04		833
LEMON John	AB	34	Edinburgh	11/5/03		484
LENHAM James	Quarter Gunner	28	Southampton	21/5/03		650
LEROSA Degora	LM		Italy	13/10/05		S946
LESSIMORE Arthur	Quarter Master	32	Aldeburgh, Suffolk	11/5/03		533
LEVER John	AB	34	Plymouth	29/11/03	Wounded in Action	778
LEVERICKS/LEVERICK Thomas	ORD	18	Norfolk	11/5/03	NGS Medal	884
LEWIS Edward	AB	22	Anglesey, Wales	11/2/04	Noted as Volunteer	827
LEWIS Jeremiah G.	Pte RM	34	Montgomery	Plymouth/30. 18/4/03	Killed in Action	M103
LEWIS John (1)	ORD	27	Baltimore, America	11/5/03		264
LEWIS John (2)	AB	29	Boston, Lincolnshire	11/5/03		416
LOFT William	ORD	22	Worcester	11/5/03		265
LONG James	Drummer RM	19		Chatham/22. 19/4/03		M128
LOVETT Samuel	AB	40	Portsmouth, America	21/5/03	Wounded in Action. Pressed	633
LOVITT Peter	Quarter Master	40	Aldeburgh, Suffolk	11/5/03		532
LOWRANE Charles	AB	53	Newton Bushell, Devon	13/8/03	Noted as Volunteer	740
LUDFORD James	Boy, 3rd class	15	Northampton	2/4/05	Wounded in Action	B3/37
LYONS John	Midshipman	21	London	5/10/04	NGS Medal. Lieut. Dec 1805	879
MAGEE John	Pte RM	40	Co Drumoore, Ireland	Chatham/43. 17/4/03		M34
MAGEE Peter	AB	21	Dublin	11/5/03		155
MAGOLINA Antonio	Pte RM	31	Naples, Italy	Chatham/61. 28/6/04	Noted as Volunteer	M173
MAINLAND William	AB	31	Orkneys, Scotland	11/5/03	NGS Medal	519
MALONEY Michael	Quarter Master's Mate	26	London	11/5/03		565
MALONEY Thomas	LM	23	Connaught, Ireland	11/5/03		139
MANN John	AB	25	Warrington, Lancashire	11/5/03		106
MANNELL William	Quarter Master's Mate	31	Aldborough, Suffolk	11/5/03	NGS Medal	530

Name	Rating	Age	Place of Birth	Date	Remarks	No.
MANNING John	ORD	29	Co. Galway, Ireland	11/5/03	NGS Medal	250
MANSELL James	AB	23	Norfolk	11/5/03	Killed in Action	78
MARAT Thomas	Supernumary			9/10/05	NGS Medal	S922
MARR Edward	AB	27	Co. Tipperary, Ireland	14/6/03		707
MARSH Henry	ORD	23	Gloucester	11/5/03	NGS Medal	205
MARSHALL John (1)	AB	22	Essex	11/5/03		352
MARSHALL John (2)	AB	44	Newcastle	11/5/03		459
MARSHALL William (1)	ORD	22	Dartmouth, Devon	11/5/03		456
MARSTON Thomas	Pte RM	16	Foleshill, Warwickshire	Portsmouth/68. 19/5/03		M152
MARTIN George	AB	28	Swansea, Wales	11/5/03	NGS Medal	290
MARTIN Samuel	ORD	25	Manchester	11/5/03	Army deserter returned to Regt	274
MASON George	AB. Supernumary	39	Hull, Yorkshire	11/10/05		S8
MASON John	Boy 2nd class. Supn.			11/10/05		S935
MASON John	AB	24	Lincoln	11/5/03		340
MATTHEWS Benjamin	Pte RM	31	Monmouthshire	Portsmouth/26. 14/6/03	Wounded in Action	M163
MATTHEWS John	AB	23	New York, America	24/10/04	Noted as Volunteer	905
MATTHEWS Robert	Pte RM	22	Cheshire	Chatham/61. 17/4/03		M61
MATTHEWS Thomas (1)	LM	25	London	11/5/03	Was detailed to Guns in action	138
MATTHEWS William	AB	41	Chilcompton, Somerset	11/10/05		979
McBETH Alexander	LM	20	Caithness	11/5/03	NGS Medal	93
McCLEMENTS Gilbert	AB	20	Ayr, Scotland	3/8/04	Pressed Man at Lisbon	896
McCONNELL John	ORD	20	Ireland	11/5/03		562
McCONNERKY Alexander	Carpenter's Crew	28	Aberdeen, Scotland	26/4/04		860
McDONALD Alexander	ORD	18	Greenock, Scotland	18/8/03	Noted as Volunteer	755
McDONALD Angus	AB	36	Inverness, Scotland	5/10/03	Wounded in Action. Pressed	784
McDONALD Archibald	ORD	21	Argylshire, Scotland	7/10/03		972
McDONALD James	AB	22	Edmonton, London	11/5/03		105
McDONALD John	AB	26	Roscrea, Tipperary, Ireland	11/5/03	Pressed Man	781
McDONALD Michael	ORD	30	Meath, Ireland	11/5/03	Wounded in Action	165
McDOWELL Alexander	ORD	25	Carrickfergus, Ireland	11/5/03		579
McELROY Thomas	Pte RM	26	Lurgan, Co Louth, Ireland	Chatham/22. 17/04/03		M72
McGUIRE Edward	AB	22	Richmond	11/5/03		158
McINDOE Archibald	ORD	22	Glasgow	3/8/04		902
McKENNAN Langhan	ORD	20	Tarbert, Scotland	11/5/03		98
McKENZIE Lewis	ORD	20	Edinburgh	11/5/03		83
McLAUGHLIN James	LM	24	Roscommon, Ireland	11/5/03		157

Name	Rank	Birthplace	Date	Notes	Number	Age
McMANNERS Owen	AB	Roscommon, Ireland	11/5/03	Killed in Action	299	28
McMANUS Bernard	Pte RM	Fermanagh	Portsmouth/8. 14/9/05	Wounded in Action	M184	26
McPHERSON Daniel	LM	Dunbarton, Scotland	11/5/03		97	20
McPHERSON James	Boy 2nd class	Shoreham, Sussex	4/5/03	From Marine Society	B2/5	16
McPHERSON Joseph	LM	Kingston on Thames	4/5/03	Wounded in Action. Volunteer	49	20
McWILLIAMS Andrew	AB	Galloway, Scotland	11/5/03		540	29
MEAD David	Pte RM	Waterford, Ireland	Chatham/82. 18/04/03		M104	41
MELEBURY/MANBURY John	Armourer's Mate	Sweden	11/5/03		370	35
MELVIN James	Pte RM	Norwich, Norfolk	Chatham/61. 17/4/03		M57	21
MERRYGAN Patrick	ORD	Waterford, Ireland	18/8/03		756	21
MIFFIN David	AB	Newcastle	11/5/03		401	27
MINUTE John	AB	Cardiff, Wales	11/5/03		335	25
MITCHELL Patrick	AB	Dundee, Scotland	11/5/03		153	45
MITCHELL William	Boy 2nd class	Staffordshire	23/4/05		B2/25	15
MITCHELL William	AB	Dundee, Scotland	2/4/05		946	56
MOLLOY Phillip	Pte RM	Dunmore, Ireland	Portsmouth/59. 14/6/03		M154	23
MONDAY/MUNDAY John	ORD	London	11/5/03	NGS Medal	475	20
MOON Simeon	AB	Bristol	11/5/03		214	23
MOONEY Edward	ORD	Dublin	21/5/03	Wounded in Action	629	38
MOORE John	Pte RM	Lancaster	Chatham/61. 17/4/03		M70	25
MORGAN John	Pte RM	Salisbury, Wiltshire	Chatham/97. 17/4/03	Wounded in Action	M45	20
MORGAN Michael	Supernumerary		9/10/05		S919	
MORLEY George	ORD	Rye, Sussex	2/4/04		849	26
MORRIS John (2)	ORD	London	11/5/03		372	18
MORRIS William	AB	London	11/5/03		346	21
MORRISON James	Armourer	New York, America	11/5/03	Originally Mustered as 448	983	39
MORTON William	AB	Fleatham, Northumberland	11/5/03	Pressed Man	602	36
MOSS John	LM	Hereford	11/5/03		571	23
MOSS John (2)	AB	London	2/4/05		953	37
MOSS Joseph	Boy 3rd class	Newington, Middlesex	23/4/04	Killed in Action	B3/31	14
MUCK William	AB	Gainsworth	11/5/03		400	20
MULLEN James S.	AB	Amsterdam, Holland	3/8/04		900	34
MUNRO Daniel	AB	Scotland	11/5/03	Wounded in Action	80	24
MURPHY John	AB	Belfast	2/4/04		847	24
MURRAY Alexander	AB	America	11/2/04	Noted as Volunteer	818	24
MURRAY Joshua	AB	Leith, Scotland	11/5/03		582	25

No.	Name	Rating	Age	Birthplace	Date	Remarks
288	MURRAY Robert	ORD	22	London	11/5/03	Killed in Action. Volunteer
M177	MYERS Lombart	Pte RM		Germany	Chatham/100. 2/9/04	
M168	NASH John	Pte RM	21	Ledbury	Portsmouth/56. 14/6/03	Wounded in Action
S918	NEALE Patrick	Supernumary			9/10/05	
1	NELSON Horatio, Lord.	Vice-Admiral	45	Burnham Thorpe, Norfok	18/5/03	Large Naval gold medal. Killed
S6	NEVILL Ralph. Hon.	AB. Supernumary	19	Sion Hill, Middlesex	10/9/05	Promoted Lieutenant 1806
M65	NICHOLLS Charles	Pte RM	21	Yarmouth, Norfolk	Chatham/67. 17/4/03	
581	NICHOLLS Henry	ORD	24	Co. Mayo, Ireland	11/5/03	NGS Medal
R7	NICHOLLS Henry	AB Retinue	21	Rhode Island, America	20/5/03	Nelson's Retinue
680	NIPPER James	AB	20	Sedbury, Gloucestershire	31/7/03	NGS Medal
M102	NORGROVE James	Pte RM	20	London	Plymouth/30. 18/4/03	Killed in Action
146	NORTH James	ORD. Signals	25	Pattingham, Staffordshire	11/5/03	Killed in Action
M48	NORTHWOOD John	Pte RM	20	Plymouth, Devon	Chatham/31. 17/4/03	
437	NORVILLE/NORVELL Robert	ORD	23	Woolwich, London	11/5/03	NGS Medal
413	NUTTING Robert	AB	22	London	11/5/03	
869	OGILVIE David	Midshipman	18	London	16/1/04	Promoted Lieutenant 1806
186	OGILVIE George	ORD	20	West Indies	11/5/03	
208	ONIONS William	ORD	20	London	11/5/03	
706	OSBORNE William	ORD	38	Liverpool	14/6/03	
358	OWEN John	AB	45	Wales	11/5/03	
359	PACKETT John/FERNIE Peter	AB	38	Havre de Grace, America	11/5/03	
498	PADARO/PARARO Francis	Quarter Gunner	24	Western Islands	11/5/03	
M172	PADDEN Edward	Pte RM	21	Modbury, Devon	Portsmouth/142. 3/8/04	Wounded in Action
644	PAGE James	AB	26	Titchfield, Hampshire	21/5/03	
491	PAIN John	LM	21	London	11/5/03	Wounded in Action
793	PAINTER Joseph	AB	21	Southampton	20/1/04	
956	PALMER Alexander	Midshipman	19	London	12/5/05	Killed in Action
M141	PALMER John	Pte RM	18	Bedfordshire	Chatham/31. 19/4/03	Killed in Action
310	PALMER Thomas	ORD	33	Surrey	11/5/03	
197	PARKE James	ORD	23	Peterhead	11/5/03	Killed in Action
909	PARKER James	ORD	23	Southampton	31/12/04	NGS Medal. Wounded.
M162	PARNELL John	Pte RM	21	Withybrook, Warwickshire	Portsmouth/86. 14/6/03	
M9	PARRY John	Pte RM		Shropshire	Chatham/88. 14/3/03	Wounded in Action

Name	Rank	Age	Place	Date	Notes	Number
PASCO John	Lieutenant of Signals	31	Devon	12/4/03	NGS Medal. Wounded	21
PATTERSON William	AB	22	Newcastle	11/5/03	Killed by mast fall, 1 Jan 1806	402
PEAKE James Godwin	1st Lieutenant RM	24	Stafford	Chatham/82. 30/4/03	Wounded in Action. Capt 1808	M149
PEARSON George	Pte RM	18	Wirksworth, Derbyshire	Chatham/61. 17/4/03		M62
PELCONE John	ORD	20	Amsterdam, Holland	11/5/03		504
PENNELL Michael	AB	42	Ipswich, Suffolk	11/2/04	Wounded in Action. Volunteer	891
PENNING Robert	Supernumary			9/10/05		S925
PENNY Alexander	AB	36	Northumberland	11/5/03		267
PEPPETT James	Boy 2nd class	15	London	23/4/04	NGS Medal	B2/22
PERCH Nathaniel/Nicholas	ORD	20	Malta	19/1/04		885
PERRION William	Boy 3rd class	13	London	27/4/03	From Marine Society	B3/18
PERRY William	Pte RM	24	Dublin	Plymouth/69. 14/4/03	Killed in Action	M13
PETERS John	AB	23	Glasgow	11/5/03		90
PETERS Valier	LM	20	London	15/4/03	Noted as Volunteer	29
PHILLIPS Robert	LM	19	Yarmouth, Norfolk	11/5/03	Wounded in Action	81
PICKERING Thomas	ORD	20	Southampton	14/6/03		713
PICKIN Oliver	Midshipman	21	Rochester, Kent	1/10/05		977
PIERCY Thomas	AB	26	Scarborough	11/2/04	Pressed Man	809
PILLE John	AB	23	Cornwall	11/5/03	NGS Medal	585
PILLIQUE Stromblo	ORD	20	Messina, Sicily	13/8/03	Noted as Volunteer	747
PITNEY Francis	Pte RM	22	Shepton Mallet, Somerset	Portsmouth/62. 14/6/03	NGS Medal	M164
PITT George	ORD	19	Bristol	21/5/03	NGS Medal. Wounded	957
POAD James	Midshipman	16	Plymouth Dock	29/4/05	NGS Medal. d. 1858	927
POLLARD John	Midshipman	18	Cawsand, Cornwall	3/4/05	NGS Medal. Wounded	932
POOLEY Isaac	ORD	21	Colchester, Essex	13/8/03	Noted as Volunteer	744
POPE William	Boy 1st class	17	Portsmouth	26/9/05	NGS Medal. Volunteer	B1/26
PORTER Abraham	Supernumary			9/10/05	NGS Medal.	S917
PORTFIELD Hugh	Boy 2nd class	14	Dublin	29/4/05		B2/29
POWELL David	Pte RM	20	Bristol	Plymouth/18. 18/4/03	NGS Medal	M99
POWELL Richard	ORD	22	Cheswick, Berwick	11/5/03	NGS Medal	127
POWELL Thomas	Pte RM	23	Monmouth	Portsmouth/29. 14/6/03		M169
PRESCOTT George	ORD	20	Hampshire	11/5/03		412
PRICE Thomas	AB	33	Shropshire	9/4/05	Wounded in Action	940
PRITCHARD Robert	ORD	21	Carnarvon, Wales	11/2/04	Noted as Volunteer	820
PRITCHARD Samuel	Pte RM	26	Chipping Sodbury, Glos.	Plymouth/39. 14/4/03		M11
PRITCHARD William	AB	25	Angelsey	11/2/04	Noted as Volunteer	825

Name	Rank/Rating	Place	Age	Date	Notes	No.
PROUT Thomas	ORD	Waterford, Ireland	38	11/5/03		477
QUILLIAM John	1st Lieutenant	Isle of Man	33	10/4/03	Awarded £5000 bounty in 1799	17
QUINTON George	Quarter Gunner	Richmond	36	14/6/03	Wounded in Action	705
RACKUM/RACKHAM John	Pte RM	Bungay, Suffolk	22	Chatham/19. 14/5/03	Killed in Action. Buried Cadiz	M151
RAM William Alexander	Lieutenant	Co. Wexford, Ireland	21	12/4/05		933
RANDALL/RANDLE Thomas	AB	Exeter, Devon	39	11/5/03	NGS Medal. d. 1851	409
RANDALL William	Boy 1st class	London	15	8/5/03	Midshipman 1806	B1/1
RAWLINS John	LM	France	23	11/5/03		474
RAWLINSON James	Boy 3rd class	Maidstone, Kent	12	17/11/03	Noted as Volunteer	B3/27
RAWLINSON Thomas	Pte RM	Chatham, Kent	37	Chatham/64. 14/4/03		M26
RAY John	ORD	Burnham, Essex	33	3/8/04	Pressed Man at Oporto	897
RAYMENT John	Pte RM	Stanford, Lincolnshire	34	Chatham/37. 19/4/03		M138
RAYNER Thomas	Pte RM	Crowland, Lincolnshire	18	Chatham/49. 14/4/03	Died of Wounds	M7
READ Daniel	ORD	London	20	11/5/03		313
RECAIN John	LM	Holland	23	11/5/03	Noted as Volunteer	63
REECE Samuel	Pte RM	Monmouthshire	29	Portsmouth/68. 18/4/03		M74
REECE William	Pte RM	Monmouth	32	Plymouth/48. 18/4/03		M111
REEVES Lewis Buckle	2nd Lieutenant RM	East Meon, Hampshire	18	Portsmouth/142. 3/8/04	NGS Medal. Wounded	M171
REMMINGTON Stephen	LM	London	37	11/5/03		536
REY John	ORD	Hornsey, Yorkshire	18	13/8/03		968
REYNOLDS/MOSER Peter	AB	London	30	11/5/03	NGS Medal is named Moser	279
RICERI Simoni	LM			13/10/05		S947
RICHARDS John	AB	Carmarthen, Wales	26	11/5/03		325
RICHARDS Samuel	AB	Tavistock, Devon	22	11/5/03		415
RICHARDS Valentine	Pte RM	Penbroke, Wales	25	Plymouth/84. 18/4/03		M124
RICHARDS William	ORD	Falmouth, Cornwall	27	13/8/03	Noted as Volunteer	746
RICHIE Peter	ORD	Dundee, Scotland	21	11/5/03		259
RIGGAN John	Supernumary			9/10/05		S921
RIVERS William	Midshipman	Portsea, Hampshire	17	4/5/03	NGS Medal. Wounded. Vol.	50
RIVERS William (1)	Gunner	Bermondsey, London	48	9/4/03		4
ROATLEY/ROTELEY Lewis	2nd Lieutenant RM	Neath, Glamorgan	20	Portsmouth/86. 3/9/05	NGS Medal. 1st Lieut. 1808	M180
ROBBINS Samuel	Boy 3rd class	London	13	2/4/05		B3/36
ROBERTS David	AB	Wales	33	11/5/03		272
ROBERTS Richard Francis	Midshipman	Burton Bradstock, Dorset	20	10/9/05	Midshipman from 19 Oct 1805	963

Name	Role	Age	Place	Date	Notes	No.
ROBERTSON/WALKER James	Midshipman	22	Stornoway, Scotland. d.1858	29/3/05	NGS Medal is named to Walker	928
ROBINS Thomas L.	Master's Mate	16	Portsmouth	27/8/03	NGS Medal. Lieut. Feb 1806	697
ROBINSON John	AB	22	Sandwich, Kent	2/4/04		837
ROE/ROWE Michael	AB	22	Dublin	11/5/03	NGS Medal	564
ROGERS James	Pte RM	30	Kilrane, Wexford, Ireland	Plymouth/45. 18/4/03	Wounded in Action	M82
ROME/ROOME John	LM	21	Battersea	11/5/03	NGS Medal. Hoisted Signal	539
ROSS John (1)	AB	40	Ross-shire, Scotland	11/5/03		225
ROSS John (2)	Quarter Gunner	35	North Britain	11/5/03		394
ROSS Robert	LM	18	Leith, Scotland	11/5/03	NGS Medal	423
ROWE James	AB	27	Plymouth Dock	21/5/03		630
ROWLAND/ROWLEY Lewis	Pte RM	21	Monmouth	Plymouth/45. 18/4/03	NGS Medal	M87
RUSSELL William	AB	57	Plymouth	11/5/03	Pressed Man	605
RYAN George	ORD	22	Africa	11/5/03		291
RYAN Stephen	LM	27	Cork, Ireland	11/5/03		203
RYLETT Henry	ORD	20	Guernsey, Channel Isles	2/4/04		832
SABINE Stephen	Boy 3rd class	13	London	27/4/03	Killed in Action. Marine Soc.	B3/8
SACK Andrew	Yeoman of Sheets	33	Geneva, Switzerland	21/5/03	Killed in Action	651
SALLAZZA Crescenzo	Pte RM	23	Naples, Italy	Chatham/100. 13/7/04	Noted as Volunteer	M176
SAMMERS John	ORD	20	Guadaloupe, West Indies	11/5/03		209
SARR James	Supernumary			9/10/05		S920
SARSON William	LM	20	Dublin	11/5/03		549
SAUNDERS Isaac	AB	20	Newport, Isle of Wight	2/4/04		842
SAUNDERS John	Boy 3rd class	14	London	27/4/03	NGS Medal. Wounded. M.Soc	B3/11
SAUNDERS/SANDERS William	AB	29	London	11/5/03	NGS Medal	156
SCATTERGOOD William	Pte RM	19	Brassington, Derbyshire	Portsmouth/77. 14/6/03		M166
SCOTT Rev. Alexander John	Chaplain	37	Rotherhithe, London	26/5/03	Nelson's Interpreter & Envoy	664
SCOTT Andrew	Sail Maker's Mate	34	Carlisle, Cumberland	13/8/03	Noted as Volunteer	738
SCOTT John	Boy 1st class	17	Highgate, Middlesex	2/4/05	Noted as Volunteer	B1/21
SCOTT John	Secretary to Nelson	35		20/5/03	Nelson's Retinue. Killed	R2
SEARCHWELL Henry	AB	21	Newcastle	14/6/03		716
SEARLE Richard	AB	28	Bath, Somerset	11/5/03		427
SECKAR James	Sergeant RM	22	Norwich, Norfolk	Chatham/97. 19/04/03		M127
SEDGWICK Thomas	Quarter Gunner	39	Sunderland	11/5/03	Carried Nelson to Cockpit	505
SELBY William	ORD	21	Dorsetshire	11/5/03		298
SEXTON Thomas	LM	30	Liverpool	11/5/03		560

Name	Rating	Age	Place	Date	Remarks	No.
SHADD Robert	LM	20	Cronarty, Scotland	11/5/03		89
SHAW William	LM	22	Birmingham	11/5/03	Killed in Action	240
SHEPPARD William	Pte RM	18	Weston, Hertfordshire	Portsmouth/47. 14/6/03	NGS Medal	M155
SHEPPARD William	LM	19	East Marlin/Mailing, Kent	5/5/03		682
SHERMAN James	ORD	19	Yarmouth, Norfolk	2/4/04	NGS Medal	834
SHIMMELL Josh	AB	37	Lincoln	11/5/03		278
SIBBALD James	Midshipman	19	Leith, Edinburgh	15/9/05	Master's Mate in Nov. 1805	965
SIMMS William	AB	21	Colchester, Essex	11/5/03		350
SIMPSON Thomas	AB	27	Leicester	11/5/03		452
SKINNER James	ORD	18	Chatham, Kent	9/5/03	Killed in Action. Volunteer	971
SKINNER William	ORD	21	Deptford, London	11/5/03		517
SKINNER William	ORD	20	Deptford, London	2/4/05	Killed in Action	943
SLOANE Andrew	Boy 2nd class. Supn.	15	Newry, Ireland	13/10/05	Noted as Volunteer	S941
SMITH Charles	Carpenter's Crew	27	Dublin	14/6/03	NGS Medal	719
SMITH David	ORD	18	Dundee, Scotland	11/5/03		485
SMITH George	Boy 2nd class	18	Forfar, Scotland	23/4/04		B2/23
SMITH George (1)	LM	20	London	11/5/03	Killed in Action	417
SMITH George (2)	AB	52	Yorkshire	11/5/03		515
SMITH James	AB	29	Cambridge, Virginia.	11/5/03		464
SMITH John (2)	ORD	28	London	11/5/03	Wounded in Action	103
SMITH John (3)	AB	25	Birchington, Kent	2/4/04		839
SMITH John	Pte RM	31	Lancashire	Chatham/49. 19/4/03		M1145
SMITH Neil	1st Assistant Surgeon			18/1/05	Made Surgeon afterTrafalgar	915
SMITH Robert	Midshipman b.1786	18	Watford, Hertfordshire	19/5/03	NGS Medal to Family. Killed	622
SMITH Thomas (1)	AB	31	London	11/5/03		309
SMITH William (1)	Sailmaker's Crew	31	Northfleet, Kent	11/5/03		328
SMITH William (2)	ORD	20	Worcester	11/5/03	Died of Wounds	483
SMITH William (4)	AB	30	South Shields	6/10/03	NGS Medal. Volunteer	803
SMITH William	Pte RM	24	Leicestershire	Chatham/13. 14/4/03		M18
SMITHSON James	AB	25	London	11/5/03	NGS Medal	566
SOUTH John	Pte RM	22	Kidderminster	Chatham/82. 18/4/03	NGS Medal	M79
SPEDILLO Gaetano	AB Valet. Retinue		Naples, Italy	20/5/03	Nelson's Retinue	R4
SPENCER Samuel	Master's Mate	24	Halifax, Yorkshire	20/8/04	NGS Medal. Lieut. 1806	866
SPENCER Thomas	Yeoman of Sheets	31	Exeter, Devon	11/5/03		317
SPENCER William (1)	Yeoman Powder Room	26	Newcastle	11/5/03		392
SPENCER William (2)	AB	24	York	11/2/04	Pressed Man	812

Name	Rating	Age	Place	Date	Notes	Number
STACEY James	ORD	44	Winchester	14/6/03		708
STAIR John	AB	26	America	11/2/04	Noted as Volunteer	815
STAKE/HAKE George	AB	25	Hull	11/5/03		248
STALLETT Andrew	AB	32	Sweden	14/6/03		725
STANFORD William	ORD	25	Brecknock	11/5/03		219
STAPLES Richard	Pte RM	18	Pattishall, Northants	Portsmouth/8. 14/9/05		M183
STAPLETON George	LM	20	London	11/5/03		369
STARR John	Quarter Gunner	26	Norwich, Norfolk	11/5/03	Pressed Man	594
STAYHAM/STRAWN Thomas	LM	18	London	11/5/03	NGS Medal	455
STEAD John	Sail Maker's Crew	40	Leeds	2/4/04		846
STEVENS Hugh	Armourer's Mate	25	London	11/5/03		238
STEVENS Samuel	LM	22	London	11/5/03	NGS Medal	111
STEVENSON Anthony	ORD	19	Rotherhithe, London	11/5/03		245
STEVENSON Benjamin	Quarter Master	22	Berwick	11/5/03		395
STEVENSON George	AB	35	Whitby	11/5/03		422
STEVENSON John	AB	30	Cork, Ireland	11/5/03		116
STEWART Charles	AB	21	Banffshire, Scotland	11/5/03	NGS Medal. Pressed Man	611
STEWART David	AB	25	Glasgow	11/2/04	Noted as Volunteer	813
STILES/STYLES Henry	LM	26	Thame, Oxfordshire	11/5/03	NGS Medal	96
STRAKER William	AB	26	York	11/5/03		282
STUDDY Francis	ORD	22	Cork, Ireland	11/2/04	Noted as Volunteer	824
SULLIVAN Cornelius	Pte RM	24	Cork, Ireland	Chatham/61. 19/4/03		M136
SULLIVAN Jeremiah	AB	22	Cork, Ireland	13/8/03	Wounded in Action. Volunteer	739
SUTHERLAND James	ORD	21	Caithness, Scotland	11/5/03	NGS Medal	373
SUTTON George	Pte RM	33	Somerset	Plymouth/51. 18/4/03		M113
SWAIN William	LM	25	Goring, Oxfordshire	9/5/03	Pressed Man	54
SWEET William	ORD	20	New York, America	27/1/04	Pressed Man	890
SYMONS William Henry	Master's Mate	22	Ashford, Kent	15/1/05	NGS Medal. Lieut. 22 Oct 1805	911
SYMS John	AB	19	Somerset	11/5/03	Wounded in Action	406
TADD William	Boy 3rd. Supernumary	19	London	11/10/05		S931
TAFT William	Corporal RM	26	Newcastle	Chatham/7. 17/4/03		M60
TART John	ORD	20	Malta	19/4/04	Wounded in Action	862
TAYLOR Alfred	AB. Signals	19	London	11/5/03	NGS Medal	173
TAYLOR George A.	LM	25	London	11/5/03	Killed in Action	166
TAYLOR William	ORD	20	Aberdeen, Scotland	11/5/03	Wounded in Action. Pressed	610

Name	Rate/Rank	Age	Place	Date	Notes	No.
TEMPLE John	LM	22	London	11/5/03		438
TERRANT/TARRANT William	Quarter Gunner	23	Isle of Wight	11/5/03	NGS Medal. Wounded	348
TERRY John	AB	24	Deal, Kent	11/5/03		367
THOMAS Charles	ORD	23	Boston, Lincolnshire	11/5/03		121
THOMAS Jeriniah	AB	25	Sussex	11/5/03		190
THOMAS John (1)	ORD	22	London	11/5/03		191
THOMAS John (2)	ORD	22	Madras, India	11/5/03		441
THOMAS Thomas/John	LM	21	Port Royal, Jamaica	11/5/03		555
THOMAS Thomas (1)	AB	21	Carnarthen, Wales	11 May 1803	Killed in Action	133
THOMPSON John	Pte RM	20	Swaffham, Cambridgeshire	Portsmouth/68. 14/6/03		M156
THOMPSON Robert	ORD	20	Shields, Yorkshire	14/6/03		717
THOMPSON Stephen	LM	20	Glasgow	11/5/03		88
THOMPSON William (1)	ORD	28	Philadelphia, America	11/5/03		141
THOMPSON William (3)	AB	22	North Shields	21/5/03	Killed in Action	631
THOMPSON William (4)	ORD	26	Boston, Lincolnshire	11/5/03	NGS Medal. Pressed Man	690
THORLING John	Quarter Master	44	Yarmouth, Norfolk	11/5/03	Noted as Volunteer	596
THOVEZ/THOREZ Philip	AB/Midshipman	20	Naples, Italy	4/10/04	Purser 1809	935
THRESHER Thomas	Midshipman	21	Waltham	3/9/05	Noted as Volunteer	960
TOBIN Richard	ORD	30	Cork, Ireland	11/5/03		377
TOMLINSON/TOMBLESON Thos.	Carpenter's Crew	22	Downham, Norfolk	11/5/03	NGS Medal	131
TOOLE Christopher	AB	25	Dublin	3/9/05		961
TUCK John	Pte RM	30	Sturminster Newton, Dorset	Portsmouth/65. 14/6/03	NGS Medal	M159
TURNER Colin	Boy 3rd class	16	Paisley, Scotland	7/10/03	Killed in Action	B3/24
TURNER Francis	LM	22	Chelsea, London	11/5/03		591
TURNER William	Corporal RM	21	Chester, Cheshire	Chatham/1. 19/4/03		M130
TWINEY Thomas	Quarter Master	26	Carnarthen, Wales	21/5/03		646
TWICHETT/TWITCHETT Thomas	Boy 3rd class	12	London	10/9/05	Noted as Volunteer	B3/39
TWITCHETT Robert	Boy 1st class	16	Hertford	27/4/03	From Marine Society	B1/25
UPTON Robert	AB	30	Suffolk	11/5/03		217
VAVA Filippo	Pte RM	23	Naples, Italy	Chatham/100. 13/7/04	Noted as Volunteer	M175
VENT James	ORD	21	London	11/5/03	Noted as Volunteer	882
VINCENT John	Quarter Gunner	28	London	11/5/03		404
WADDLE William	LM	20	Glasgow	11/5/03		85

Name	Rating	Age	Place	Date	Notes	No.
WALKER Alexander	AB	20	Wiltshire	11/2/04	Killed in Action. Volunteer	810
WALKER George	ORD	23	Carmarthen, Wales	3/8/04	Pressed Man at Gibraltar	903
WALKER John	AB	32	London	11/5/03		307
WALKER Samuel	Pte RM	20	Worcester	Plymouth/69. 18/04/03		M91
WALTON John	LM	23	Leith	11/5/03		82
WALTON William	LM	29	Kenningsworth	11/5/03		143
WARD Edward	Pte RM	30	Hereford	Portsmouth/65. 14/6/03	NGS Medal	M158
WARD George	Boy 3rd class. Supn.	15	Manchester	13/10/05	NGS Medal.	S944
WARD Joseph	ORD	20	Hereford	2/4/05	Killed in Action	952
WARDEN Alexander	AB	26	Plymouth	11/5/03		181
WARNER James	Pte RM	18	Chelmsford, Essex	Chatham/61. 17/4/03		M63
WARRUNDALL John	AB	22	Boston, Lincolnshire	14/6/03		762
WATERS Charles	AB	25	Monmouth	11/5/03		213
WATERS Edward	AB	24	Hertford, Hertfordshire	11/5/03	Killed in Action	563
WATERS William	ORD	24	London	11/5/03		381
WATSON Thomas	AB	31	Northfleet, Kent	11/5/03		351
WEBSTER William	AB. Supernumary	21	Norwich, Norfolk	2/10/05		S7
WELLAN John	AB	22	Holland	11/5/03		324
WELLS William	Pte RM	26	Goudhurst, Kent	Chatham/52. 19/04/03	Wounded in Action	M134
WELSH John (1)	LM	26	Waterford, Ireland	11/5/03		287
WELSH John (2)	AB	20	Edinburgh	2/4/04	Killed in Action	851
WELSH William	LM	20	Crayford, Kent	11/5/03	Wounded in Action	262
WELSTEAD John	Boswain's Mate	36	Milton Abbey, Dorset	21/5/03		654
WEST James	LM	20	Faversham, Kent	11/5/03	NGS Medal. Volunteer	68
WEST Richard (1)	AB	31	Faversham, Kent	11/5/03	Noted as Volunteer	69
WESTENBURGH William	Surgeon's 2nd Mate			16 March 1805	Warrant of 16 March 1805	923
WESTPHAL George A.	Midshipman	19	Lambeth, London. d 1875	31/7/03	NGS Medal. Wounded	671
WHARTON John	ORD	28	Hackney, London	11/5/03	Killed in Action	446
WHICH/ULRICK Peter	ORD	22	Stockholm, Sweden	20/1/04		792
WHIPPLE Thomas	Captain's Clerk	18	Plymouth	31/7/03	Killed in Action	667
WHITE Richard	LM	20	London	11/5/03		188
WHITE William	Supn. Boy 3rd class	18	Dublin	11/10/05	Also listed as B3/42	S932
WHITE William	AB	20	Plymouth	11/5/03		320
WHITTON/BITTON John	LM	21	Freethorpe, Norfolk	11/5/03	Noted as Volunteer	598
WHITTON/BITTON Thomas	Carpenter's Crew	20	Freethorpe, Norfolk	11/5/03	Noted as Volunteer	599
WILKES Samuel	Pte RM	21	Birmingham	Plymouth/66. 17/4/03	Killed in Action	M49

Name	Rating	Age	Place	Date	Notes	No.
WILKINS George	AB	38	Surrey	14/6/03		715
WILKINS Henry	ORD	23	Bristol	11/5/03		76
WILKINSON Benjamin	ORD	20	London	11/5/03		132
WILLIAMS Edward	Lieutenant	38	Dorset	25/1/04	Promoted Commander 1805	796
WILLIAMS James	AB	22	Liverpool	14/6/03		723
WILLIAMS John (3)	AB	32	Chester	27/1/04		805
WILLIAMS John (4)	ORD	23	Reading, Berkshire	2/4/05		944
WILLIAMS Richard	ORD	23	Beaumaris, Wales	11/2/04	Noted as Volunteer	822
WILLMET William	Boatswain 14/3/1805			29/3/05	Wounded in Action	926
WILLMOTT George	Pte RM	23	Downhead, Somerset	Plymouth/30. 18/4/03	Killed in Action	M100
WILLOUGHBY Thomas	LM	32	Lincolnshire	11/5/03		167
WILSON George	Boy 2nd class	15	Bristol	27/4/03	Killed in Action. Marine Soc.	B2/4
WILSON William	LM	35	Lancaster	11/5/03		202
WILTON Thomas	Pte RM	23		Plymouth/33. 14/4/03	Wounded in Action	M25
WINNIGLE William	AB	38	Malden, Essex	11/5/03		451
WISE Edward	AB	25	Whitstable, Kent	13/10/05	NGS Medal	980
WITCHALL Christopher	Pte RM	21	Gloucester	Portsmouth/77. 14/6/03		M157
WIZZEN/WIZEN George	Pte RM	21		Portsmouth/29. 14/6/03	NGS Medal	M161
WOOD Thomas (1)	ORD	23	London	11/5/03		252
WOOD Thomas (2)	AB	40	Washington, Co Durham	11/5/03	Pressed Man	606
WOOD William (1)	ORD	24	Stens, Yorkshire	11/5/03		123
WOOD William (3)	LM	27	London	11/5/03		421
WORSON Thomas	Boy 3rd class	15	London	27/4/03	Marine Society boy	B3/12
WRIGHT James	Boatswain's Mate	28	London	20/1/04	Wounded in Action	791
WRIGHT William	Pte RM	26	Cambridgeshire	Chatham/4. 14/4/03		M14
YAULE Hans	LM	20	Switzerland	11/5/03		523
YULE John	Lieutenant	25	Plymouth	10/4/03	Promoted Commander 1805	20

Total of Ship's Company listed is 822.
This includes 145 Royal Marine officers and men

A List of those officers and men
killed and wounded
on
HMS VICTORY
at TRAFALGAR

Nelson & Bronte (signature)

"England expects that every man will do his duty"

Nelson's signal to the Fleet, 11.40am, 21st October 1805

CONFIRMED CASUALTIES, HMS VICTORY, 21st OCTOBER 1805

Casualty figures relating to the crew of *HMS Victory* for Trafalgar, have been set out in various works, usually the stark figures of 57 killed and 75 wounded, sometimes the officers and warrant officers are noted by name, with the other ranks shown as a total figure, either "killed in action" or "wounded".

To set out the names of everyone who was killed on *Victory* during the Trafalgar action or died later from his wounds was not a problem. To set out a roll of all the wounded was a little more difficult, some men claimed to have been wounded at Trafalgar, but their claims were made many years after the battle, when perhaps memories had lapsed. Even Admiral W. W. Percival Johnson in a report published in *The Graphic*, March 1879, said he had been on board the flagship during the Trafalgar action, which was unfortunately not true. So all these late claims had to be treated with some degree of caution. After much research, I now feel the enclosed casualty roll is as accurate as today's research will allow.

To this end I have combed through the numbered wound tickets entered by the ship's clerk in *Victory's* Muster Table, (ADM36-15900). Also consulted was the list of seriously wounded men disembarked on 29th October 1805, at Gibraltar, these men were entered in the Naval Hospital Ledger at Gibraltar, (ADM 102/232). A reliable source to confirm the names of officers and men who received monetry awards for their wounds, is of course the provider of such rewards, Lloyd's Patriotic Fund. The details of those who received wound payments is set out in the Lloyd's Patriotic Fund, Third Report 1806. This listing of wounded men and their rewards has been incorporated into this roll.

The Trafalgar casualty report given by Admiral Lord Collingwood to the Admiralty Office and printed in the London Gazette Extraordinary, 27 November 1805, page 1483. States casualties for *Victory*. "4 Officers, 3 Petty Officers, 32 Seamen and 18 Marines killed; 4 Officers, 3 Petty Officers, 59 Seamen and 9 Marines, wounded. - Total 132." (57 killed and 75 wounded). On page 1484 of this same London Gazette, the names of the officers who were killed or wounded appear, the report also lists the Captain's clerk as killed and the Agent Victualler's clerk as wounded.

These figures were supplied by Surgeon William Beatty to Captain Hardy soon after the battle. It fell to Beatty, his Assistant Surgeon Neil Smith and Surgeon's Mate William Westerburgh, to note the casulties, they had operated on and treated in the cramped confines below deck, all in appalling bloody conditions. So it was no wonder that some less seriously injured men never presented themselves, and therefore did not appear in the original casualty report. Boatswain William Willmet who received a painful injury to his thigh, bound up the wound himself and never left his post during the battle. All those killed during the action were immediately thrown overboard to clear the decks of obstructions, the only exception being Lord Nelson. The dead who were consigned to the sea, were noted by Captain Hardy who instructed the clerk to enter the ominous "DD" against their names in the Muster Table. Also entered were the men who died of their wounds in the following days before *Victory* reached Gibraltar, these men were also 'buried at sea'.

One man was buried twice, Lieutenant William Ram killed during the thick of the action was hastily 'buried at sea', only to be washed up later on the Spanish coast. His corpse was found by some English prisoners of war who identified Ram by the clothes he was wearing. They obtained permission from the Governor of Cadiz, to give the body of Lieutenant William Ram a decent Christian burial at Cadiz.

It was neccessary for each ship to furnish details of damage and casualty figures as soon as possible, so as to enable the new Commander in Chief, Vice-Admiral Collingwood, to appraise the state of the Fleet. The casualty figures were handed over at Gibraltar on the 29th of October. In William Beatty's narative published after the battle, he mentions that after the casualty report had been despatched, a further twenty seven men from *Victory* reported themselves wounded.

As the Naval Hospital at Gibraltar was meticulous with records, I am confident that the Hospital entry ledger can be relied upon to reflect all casualties treated in this establishment. Like any naval ship the hospital was obliged to substantiate any claim for drawing victuals against each patient lodged in their care. The Gibraltar Hospital had 581 Trafalgar wounded receiving treatment at this time.

Lloyd's Fund Committee consulted Admiralty Office reports and London Gazette action reports, this enabled the Committee to identify those considered worthy recipients of the valuable Patriotic Fund money. The needs of the wounded, the distressed families of those who perished during the battle, would then be addressed.

If a man does not appear listed as wounded in any of these four sources, *Victory's* Muster Table, Gibraltar Hospital Entry Ledger, The London Gazette Extraordinary 27 November 1805, or Lloyd's Third Report 1806, one should treat such additional claims with some caution but not entirely with scepticism. I have included amongst the wounded John Pollard, Midshipman and Charles Chappell, Master's Mate, together with another fifteen men, all of whom were recorded as wounded some while after the battle, but did not receive official recognition of their wounds at the time, or subsequently by Lloyd's Patriotic Fund wound payments. These men appear at the end of the Casualty Roll under the heading: "Not confirmed".

On the 29th of October 1805, *Victory* reached Gibraltar where the badly wounded men were transferred to the Naval Hospital for treatment. The entry ledger states that four men from the *Victory* eventually died of their wounds and were interred at that place. The last man from the *Victory* to die of his wounds in the Naval Hospital, was Royal Marine William Knight who was "discharged dead" on the 2nd of December 1805, being buried at Gibraltar. Thus the final figure of those who died reached 61.

Fourteen of the wounded men from *Victory* survived to be awarded the Naval General Service Medal, clasp TRAFALGAR. The NGS roll also includes the two officers placed at the end of the Casualty roll under "Not confirmed". These officers claimed in later years to have suffered wounds at Trafalgar. This claim was reinforced when submitting their written biographical naval services to William O'Byrne for his 1849 monumental work: *A Naval Biographical Dictionary*.

OFFICERS AND MEN KILLED IN ACTION

Name and Rank as shown in Victory's Muster Table	Casualty Ticket	Muster Number	Casualty Details
NELSON Horatio, Vice-Admiral	530	S1	Discharged Dead
ADAIR Charles William, Captain RM	550	M1	Discharged Dead
PALMER Alexander, Midshipman	513	956	DD. Died 28 Oct. 1805
RAM William Alexander, Lieut. RN	509	933	Discharged Dead
SCOTT John, Secretary to Nelson	529	S2	Discharged Dead
SMITH Robert, Midshipman	510	622	Discharged Dead
WHIPPLE Thomas, Captain's Clerk	581	667	Discharged Dead
BERRY James, Drummer RM	548	M5	Discharged Dead
BOWLER John, LM	571	311	Discharged Dead
BRENNAN John, Pte RM	542	M96	Discharged Dead
BROWN John (1), Pte RM	547	M112	Discharged Dead
BROWN William (1) AB	570	339	Discharged Dead
COBOURNE William, Pte RM	536	M42	Discharged Dead
COCKRAN George, Corporal RM	549	M85	Discharged Dead
CORWARDER John, ORD	563	572	Discharged Dead
CRAMWELL Henry, LM	532	263	DD. Died 26 Oct. 1805
DANIELS Thomas, LM	579	125	Discharged Dead
DAVIS Charles (1), ORD	572	295	Discharged Dead
DAVISON Robert, AB	565	520	Discharged Dead
EBBSWORTH John, Pte RM	537	M15	Discharged Dead
GORDON Joseph, ORD	531	973	DD. Died 27 Oct. 1805
GREEN James, Pte RM	528	M51	Discharged Dead
HERWIN Arthur, ORD	558	845	Discharged Dead
HILLIER Daniel, Pte RM	543	M114	Discharged Dead
JEWELL Richard, ORD	573	251	Discharged Dead
JOHNSON Thomas, Quarter Master	561	640	Discharged Dead
JONES William, Pte RM	535	M115	Discharged Dead
KENNEDY George, Pte RM	544	M53	Discharged Dead
KING John, Quarter Master/Yeo Sig.	566	508	Discharged Dead
LEWIS Jeremiah G. Pte RM	540	M103	Discharged Dead
McMANUS Bernard, Pte RM	538	M184	Discharged Dead
MANSELL James, AB	580	78	Discharged Dead
MUCK William, AB	569	400	Discharged Dead
MYERS Lombart, Pte RM	546	M177	Discharged Dead
NORGROVE James, Pte RM	541	M102	Discharged Dead
NORTH James, ORD	577	146	Discharged Dead
PALMER John, Pte RM	533	M141	Discharged Dead
PARKE James, ORD	575	197	Discharged Dead
PERRY William, Pte RM	534	M13	Discharged Dead
SABINE Stephen, Boy 3rd class	552	B3/8	Discharged Dead
SACK Andrew, Yeoman of Sheets	560	651	Discharged Dead
SHAW William, LM	574	240	Discharged Dead
SKINNER James, ORD	554	971	Discharged Dead
SKINNER William, ORD	556	943	Discharged Dead
SMITH George (1), LM	568	417	Discharged Dead
TAYLOR Alfred, AB	576	173	Discharged Dead
THOMAS Thomas (1), AB	578	133	Discharged Dead
THOMPSON William (3), AB	562	631	Discharged Dead
TURNER Colin, Boy 3rd class	551	B3/24	Discharged Dead
WALKER Alexander, AB	559	810	Discharged Dead
WARD Joseph, ORD	555	952	Discharged Dead
WATERS Edward, AB	564	563	Discharged Dead
WELSH John (2), AB	557	851	Discharged Dead
WHARTON John, ORD	567	446	Discharged Dead

WILKES Samuel, Pte RM	545		M49	Discharged Dead
WILLMOTT George, Pte RM	539		M100	Discharged Dead
WILSON George, Boy 2nd class	553		B2/4	Discharged Dead

DANGEROUSLY WOUNDED OFFICERS AND MEN

Name and Rank as show in Victory's Muster Table	Casualty Ticket	Lloyd's Award	Muster Number	
PASCO John, Signal Lieutenant		£100	21	Grape-shot in right side
RIVERS William, Midshipman		£80	50	Left leg shattered by shot
ANDERSON Hans, AB	494	£20	786	Compound fracture
BUCHAN David, AB	499	£40	330	Leg shattered, amputated
BURGESS James, Pte RM	486	£40	M165	Leg shattered, amputated
BURGIN Joseph, ORD	498	£40	269	Left leg shattered by shot
BUSH John, ORD	491	£20	221	Gunshot wound
COOKE Benjamin, Pte RM	475	£20	M88	DD Gibraltar 5 Nov 1805
DEANE Nicholas, Pte RM	434	£20	M86	Gunshot wound
GREGORY John, Pte RM		£20	M50	
HINES James, Pte RM	478	£20	M120	Compound fracture
JONES William (3), LM	497	£40	829	Leg amputated
KNIGHT William, Pte RM	480	£20	M116	DD Gibraltar 2 Dec 1805
LEVER John, AB	487		778	Severe leg wound, Gibraltar
MATTHEWS Benjamin, Pte RM	476	£20	M163	Gunshot wound
McPHERSON Daniel, LM	500	£20	97	Compound fracture
RAYNER Thomas, Pte RM	483	£20	M7	DD Gibraltar 20 Nov 1805
SAUNDERS John, Boy 3rd class	486	£20	B3/11	Gunshot wound
SMITH John (2), ORD	493	£20	103	Gunshot wound
SMITH William (2), ORD	495		483	DD Gibraltar 3 Nov 1805
TAFT William, Corporal RM	482	£40	M60	Arm shattered, amputated
WELLS William, Pte RM	479	£40	M134	Arm shattered, amputated
WILTON Thomas, Pte RM	477	£20	M25	Compound fracture

BADLY WOUNDED OFFICERS AND MEN

BLIGH George Miller, Lieutenant, RN		£100	19	Musket ball to the head
REEVES Lewis Buckle, 2nd Lieut. RM		£50	M171	Wounded by deck shot
BURTON George, ORD		£20	242	
CASTLE William, AB	496	£20	966	Gunshot wound
DARNOLD William, Ord		£20	425	
DICKSON John, LM	474		428	
DRUCE Edward, ORD		£20	950	
FRANCOIS John, ORD		£20	695	
GREEN Thomas (1), AB	490	£20	652	Gunshot wound
HALL Peter, LM		£20	52	
HONNOR William, Quarter Gunner	489	£20	59	Gunshot wound
PADDEN Edward, Pte RM	485	£20	M172	Gunshot wound
PAIN John, LM	473		491	
PARKER James, ORD	492	£20	909	Foot wound
SULLIVAN Jeremiah, AB	488	£20	739	Gunshot wound to knee

SLIGHTLY WOUNDED OFFICERS AND MEN

PEAKE James Godwin, 1st Lieut. RM		£30	M149	
BULKELEY Richard, Midshipman		£25	677	
WESTPHAL George A. Midshipman		£25	671	In cockpit with head wound
GEOGHEGAN John, Agent Victlr Clerk		£25	S911	
BOMKWORTH John, ORD		£10	906	
BROWN Launcelot, Yeoman Pdr Room		£25	403	
BUTLER William, AB		£10	192	

Name and Rank as shown in Victory's Muster Table	Lloyd's Award	Muster Number	
CHAPPELL Charles, Pte RM	£10	M24	
COLLARD Thomas, AB	£10	659	
CONN David, LM	£10	61	
COOPER Samuel, AB	£10	714	
COULSTON George, Pte RM	£10	M12	
CROFTON Thomas, Pte RM	£10	M19	
CURRY James, AB	£10	343	
DUTTON John, Pte RM	£10	M81	
FALL William, AB	£10	732	
FEAGAN James, Pte RM	£10	M36	
GIBSON Robert, AB	£10	154	
GILLETT William, ORD	£10	420	
GRAHAM Thomas, ORD	£10	970	
GRAVES George, Pte RM	£10	M77	
GREEN Samuel, Pte RM	£10	M135	
GREY Edward, ORD	£10	486	
GUINTI Giovanni, Pte RM	£10	M170	
HARRIS Isaac, Pte RM	£10	M117	
KENTALL John, ORD	£10	283	
LE COUTEUR/COUTH Nicholas, AB	£10	S936	
LEARY Daniel, AB	£10	275	
LEGG Charles, LM	£10	243	
LOVETT Samuel, AB	£10	633	
McDONALD Angus, AB	£10	784	
McDONALD Michael, ORD	£10	165	
McPHERSON Joseph, LM	£10	49	
MUNRO Daniel, AB	£10	80	
NASH John, Pte RM	£10	M168	
PENNELL Michael, AB	£10	891	
PHILLIPS Robert, LM	£10	81	
PRICE Thomas, AB	£10	940	
QUINTON George, Quarter Gunner	£10	705	
ROGERS James, Pte RM	£10	M82	
SYMS John, AB	£10	406	
TAYLOR William, ORD	£10	610	
WILLMET William, Boatswain	£30	926	Gunshot wound to thigh
WRIGHT James, Boatswain's Mate	£25	791	

WOUNDED NOT CONFIRMED BY LLOYD'S AWARDS

POLLARD John, Midshipman		932	Splinter in right arm
BLAKE David, AB		399	
BOND William, AB		256	
CASWELL John, ORD		838	
CHAPPELL Charles, Master's Mate		928	Sustained facial wounds
GODBY Philip, AB		939	
HAGGERTY Thomas, AB		334	
HALL William, AB		460	
HANNAM William, ORD		808	
HARRIS George, AB		177	
LUDFORD James, Boy 3rd class		B3/37	
MOONEY Edward, ORD		629	
MORGAN John, Pte RM		M45	
PARRY John, Pte RM		M9	
PITT George, ORD		957	
TERRANT William, Quarter Gunner		348	
WELSH William, LM		262	

NAVAL HOSPITAL GIBRALTAR, ENTRY LEDGER 1805.

ADM 102/232

The following details have been taken from the Entry Ledger once held at the Naval Hospital Gibraltar. The dangerously wounded men were received at the hospital from *HMS Victory* on the 29th of October 1805. The treatment for the majority was completed in six days. Those with serious wounds and amputations were gradually discharged over the following weeks. The 2 men listed at the end of this roll, John PAIN and John DICKSON, although slightly wounded, were detailed to accompany the seriously wounded to the Gibraltar Hospital as attendant helpers.

Name	Rank	Muster	Injury sustained and other Details
ANDERSON Hans	AB	786	Compound fracture
BUCHAN David	AB	330	Amputate leg
BURGESS James	Pte RM	M165	Amputate leg
			63 days in hospital, discharged 29/1/1806
BURGIN Joseph	ORD	269	Amputate left thigh, discharged 2/1/1806
BUSH John	ORD	221	Gunshot wound
CASTLE William	AB	966	Gunshot wound
COOKE Benjamin	Pte RM	M88	Gunshot wound and compound fractures
			DD. 5 November 1805. Interred at Gibraltar
DEAN Nicholas	Pte RM	M86	Gunshot wound
GREEN Thomas (1)	AB	652	Gunshot wound
HINES James	Pte RM	M120	Compound fracture
HONNOR William	Qtr Gunner	59	Gunshot wound
JONES William (3)	LM	829	Amputate leg
KNIGHT William	Pte RM	M116	Compound fracture
			DD. 2 December 1805. Interred at Gibraltar
LEVER John	AB	778	Leg wound
McPHERSON Daniel	LM	97	Compound fracture
			63 days in hospital, discharged 29/1/1806
MATTHEWS Benjamin	Pte RM	M163	Gunshot wound
PADDEN Edward	Pte RM	M172	Gunshot wound
PARKER James	ORD	909	Foot wound
RAYNER Thomas	Pte RM	M7	Gunshot wound
			DD 20 November 1805. Interred at Gibraltar
SAUNDERS John	Boy 3rd	B3/11	Gunshot wound
SMITH John (2)	ORD	103	Gunshot wound
SMITH William (2)	ORD	483	Amputate thigh
			DD. 3 November 1805. Interred at Gibraltar
SULLIVAN Jeremiah	AB	739	Gunshot wound to knee
TAFT William	Cpl RM	M60	Amputate arm
WELLS William	Pte RM	M134	Amputate arm
WILTON Thomas	Pte RM	M25	Compound fracture
PAIN John	LM	491	Slightly wounded, also acted as attendant
DICKSON John	LM	428	Slightly wounded, also acted as attendant
			Both received on 30th October, six days stay

DD indicates that the man was discharged dead.

TREATMENT AND CARE FOR THE BATTLE WOUNDED

The badly wounded men who needed to be taken to the cockpit had to be man handled down flights of steps that led into the cockpit, it invariably took at least two seamen to accomplish this angonising journey, and carry the man's poor shattered body below. Once in the cockpit wounded men waited their turn for the surgeon's attention, a strict code was enforced, status or rank were forgotten, men were treated in order according to their time of arrival in the cockpit, regardless of rank.

During the battle the cockpit was a place of frantic efforts to save life, it was also a place of bloody horror. Men in a pitiful state of injury cried out for the surgeon's attention, those near to death prayed for life and forgiveness. Others passively awaited what was in store for them.

Victory's Surgeon William Beaty and his Assistant Surgeon Neil Smith together with the Surgeon's Mate William Westerburgh, worked tirelessly to repair the damaged bodies that arrived in a quick succession. The surgeons had two untrained assistants, known as 'loblolly boys', these men helped with the operations, and held the men down during the neccessary probing and cutting. They also carried the injured men forward in correct order of appearance, to the surgeons for treatment. Wounded men were brought below to the cockpit by their comrades, who were expected to return to their stations immediately after placing the man in the surgeon's care. Marine sentries were placed on the hatchways to the cockpit, this to prevent other men from taking refuge below from enemy shot.

William Rivers a young Midshipman was carried down the steps into the cockpit, his left leg shattered by shot. The surgeon took the saw and cut the young man's leg bone off, four inches below the knee. The Midshipman fully conscious felt the injured stump and asked the surgeon "what have you left me?" It so happened his father served on the ship as the Gunner. When the action was over William Rivers the Gunner, went down to the cockpit to enquire after his son, straining in the gloom to find the young man amongst the lines of wounded, he was startled to hear a bright voice call out on the far side of the cockpit, "Here I am father, nothing is the matter with me, only lost my leg and that in a good cause". The Midshipman asked the surgeon if he could be allowed to leave the cockpit with his father, the surgeon agreed. The Gunner took his boy back to his cabin and settled him down for the night, at about midnight the Midshipman awoke at the sound of movement on the portside, he asked his father "are they throwing arms and legs overboard"? This was a surgeons practice, always done after dark, "yes" came the reply, "have they thrown nine," "I don't know" was the answer. William Rivers with one leg, was commissioned a Lieutenant on 8th January 1806, a promotion gained for his part in the battle, he lived to serve the Royal Navy for many years and died at the Royal Hospital Greenwich, aged 78 years.

Joseph Burgin, had earlier in his naval career served on Nelson's flagship the *Vanguard* at the Battle of the Nile. Now on the *Victory* at Trafalgar, Joseph Burgin was stationed on the 13th gun on the middle deck, when a shot from the French *Bucentaure* crashed through and smashed his left leg. Taken to the surgeon, Burgin had his leg amputated high up on the thigh. He was one of the wounded taken to the Naval Gibraltar Hospital, after weeks of care he was placed aboard the Hospital Ship *Sussex* on 2 January, for passage home, reaching England on 18 January. His peg leg was made famous by a piece of Staffordshire Pottery depicting this old sailor.

The Death of Nelson in Victory's Cockpit.

The wounded Admiral is represented laid on a pallet, on the larboard side of the cockpit, with pious resignation in his dying moments, his hand in Captain Hardy's. Mr. Burke, the purser, in a reclining posture in front, is supporting him with pillows. The Rev. Dr. Scott, the chaplain, is behind supporting his head. Mr. Beatty, the surgeon, having his right hand with a hankerchief placed on the wound, expresses in his countenance that vital spark is almost extinguished. Next to him stands Mr. Smith, the assistant surgeon, apparently listening to the last words articulated by the dying Hero, namely, "I have done my duty - I praise God for it." The carpenter's mate is represented on the foreground to the left of the picture in a stooping attitude, stepping over the coil of cables. Mr. Bunce, the carpenter, is standing near the cockpit ladder, with a mallet in his hand. Henry Chevallier, Nelson's faithful steward, is represented in a dejected attitude looking on, and holding his master's hat and coat. Next to him, on his left, stands Gaetano Spedillo, Nelson's valet.

The original painting was by Benjamin West, this engraving was executed by R. Golding in 1808.

The Lloyd's Patriotic Fund £100 Trafalgar sword, awarded to Richard Grindall, Captain of HMS Prince.

Label from the inside lid of a Patriotic Fund sword box, explaining its symbolism. The swords were made by Richard Teed of Lancaster Court, Strand.

Patriotic Fund vase, presented to Sophia Duff, widow of Captain George Duff who was killed in the Battle of Trafalgar. The vase is inscribed "in memory of George Duff Esquire, Captain of HMS Mars".

LLOYD'S PATRIOTIC FUND SWORDS & VASES AWARDED FOR THE BATTLE OF TRAFALGAR

TWENTY-THREE ROYAL NAVAL OFFICERS RECEIVED A £100 TRAFALGAR SWORD

Captain Israel PELLEW. *Conqueror*, 74 guns.
Captain Henry William BAYNTUN. *Leviathan*, 74 guns.
Lieutenant John PILFOLD, (Acting Captain). *Ajax*, 74 guns.
Captain Charles John Moore MANSFIELD. *Minotaur*, 74 guns.
Captain Sir Francis LAFOREY, Bart. *Spartiate*, 74 guns.
Captain Charles BULLEN. *Britannia*, 100 guns.
Captain Henry DIGBY. *Africa*, 64 guns.
Captain Charles TYLER. *Tonnant*, 80 guns.
Lieutenant William PRYCE CUMBY, (Acting Captain). *Bellerophon*, 74 guns.
Captain Sir Richard KING, Bart. *Achille*, 74 guns.
Captain Robert REDMILL. *Polyphemus*, 64 guns.
Captain Robert MOORSOM. *Revenge*, 74 guns.
Captain William George RUTHERFORD. *Swiftsure*, 74 guns.
Captain George Johnstone HOPE. *Defence*, 74 guns.
Lieutenant John STOCKHAM, (Acting Captain). *Thunderer*, 74 guns.
Captain Philip Charles DURHAM. *Defiance*, 74 guns.
Captain Richard GRINDALL. *Prince*, 98 guns.
Captain John CONN. *Dreadnought*, 98 guns.
Captain The Hon Henry BLACKWOOD. *Euryalus*, Frigate.
Captain William PROWSE. *Sirius*, Frigate.
Captain Thomas DUNDAS. *Naiad*, Frigate.
Lieutenant John Richard LAPENOTIERE. *Pickle*, Schooner.
Lieutenant Robert Benjamin YOUNG. *Entreprenante*, Cutter.

FIFTEEN PATRIOTIC FUND SILVER VASES WERE PRESENTED FOR TRAFALGAR

£500 vase to Lady Viscountess Nelson for Vice-Admiral NELSON. *Victory*, 100 guns
£500 vase to Earl Nelson for Vice-Admiral NELSON. *Victory*, 100 guns.
£500 vase to Vice-Admiral Cuthbert COLLINGWOOD. *Royal Sovereign*, 100 guns.
£300 vase to Rear-Admiral the Earl of NORTHESK. *Britannia*, 100 guns..
£200 vase to Mrs. Cooke for Captain John COOKE, killed in action. *Bellerophon*, 74
£100 vase to Captain Thomas Masterman HARDY. *Victory*, 100 guns.
£100 vase to CaptainThomas Francis FREMANTLE. *Neptune*, 98 guns.
£100 vast to Captain Sir Edward BERRY, Kt. *Agamemnon*, 64 guns.
£100 vase to Captain Edward ROTHERAM. *Royal Sovereign*, 100 guns.
£100 vase to Mrs. Duff for Captain George DUFF, killed in action. *Mars*, 74 guns.
£100 vase to Lieutenant William HENNAH. *Mars*, 74 guns.
£100 vase to Captain William HARGOOD. *Belleisle*, 74 guns.
£100 vase to Captain James Nicoll MORRIS. *Colossus*, 74 guns.
£100 vase to Mr Simens for Lieut.Thomas SIMENS, killed in action. *Defiance*, 74 guns
£100 gilt vase to Captain the Hon. Thomas BLADEN CAPEL. *Phoebe*, Frigate.

Captain Eliab Harvey of the *Temeraire* and Captain Edward Codrington of *Orion* were voted £100 swords by Lloyd's Patriotic Committee, but these officers requested alternative rewards.

NAVAL GOLD MEDALS AWARDED FOR TRAFALGAR

ADMIRALS AWARDED THE NAVAL LARGE GOLD MEDAL

NELSON, Viscount K.B., Vice-Admiral. *Victory* Posthumously to family
COLLINGWOOD, Cuthbert, Vice-Admiral. *Royal Sovereign*
NORTHESK, William, Earl of, Rear-Admiral. *Britannia*

OFFICERS AWARDED THE NAVAL SMALL GOLD MEDAL

Captain Henry William BAYNTUN. *Leviathan*
Captain Sir Edward BERRY, Kt. *Agamemnon*
Captain Charles BULLEN. *Britannia*
Captain Edward CODRINGTON. *Orion*
Captain John CONN. *Dreadnought*
Captain John COOKE. Posthumously *Bellerophon*
Captain Henry DIGBY. *Africa*
Captain George DUFF. Posthumously *Mars*
Captain Philip Charles DURHAM. *Defiance*
Captain Thomas Francis FREMANTLE. *Neptune*
Captain Richard GRINDALL. *Prince*
Captain Thomas Masterman HARDY. *Victory*
Captain William HARGOOD. *Belleisle*
Captain Eliab HARVEY. *Temeraire*
Captain George Johnstone HOPE. *Defence*
Captain Sir Richard KING, Bart. *Achille*
Captain Sir Francis LAFOREY, Bart. *Spartiate*
Captain Charles John Moore MANSFIELD. *Minotaur*
Captain Robert MOORSOM. *Revenge*
Captain James Nicoll MORRIS. *Colossus*
Captain Israel PELLEW. *Conqueror*
Lieutenant John PILFOLD. (Acting Captain). *Ajax*
Captain Robert REDMILL. *Polyphemus*
Captain Edward ROTHERAM. *Royal Sovereign*
Captain William George RUTHERFORD. *Swiftsure*
Lieutenant John STOCKHAM. (Acting Captain). *Thunderer*
Captain Charles TYLER. *Tonnant*

At the head of the page opposite are shown the Naval Large Gold Medal obverse and reverse.
Centre of page the Naval Small Gold Medal obverse with buckle on chest ribbon.
Foot of the page, the reverse of two Naval Small Gold Medals, the right hand medal was awarded to
Richard Grindall, Captain of HMS Prince at Trafalgar.

THE NAVAL GENERAL SERVICE MEDAL 1793-1840
FOR TRAFALGAR

The clasp Trafalgar to the Naval General Service Medal commemorates one of the most important and historic fleet actions ever fought by the British Navy. To be able to confirm that a recipient of a Trafalgar medal had served as a crew member on the flagship *HMS Victory*, makes the connection with history all the more poignant. The recipient of this medal with clasp Trafalgar had fought in Britain's greatest naval victory, and had the honour to serve under the immediate command of the most celebrated naval hero of all time, - Lord Horatio Nelson.

The *Naval War Medal*, as it was originally known, would to be awarded to the veterans of specific naval battles that took place between the years 1793 and 1840. In the case of the Battle of Trafalgar, it took 42 years before Parliament finally honoured Nelson's gallant sailors with this award. So many years had passed between the battle and the issuance of the medal in 1848, it was no wonder that the fleet that numbered over 18,000 souls in 1805, was dramatically reduced to a little over 1,700 claimants for the Trafalgar clasp to the Naval General Service Medal.

Any sailor who was known to have served on the *Victory* with Nelson at his last battle, was considered a worthy hero in his own right, he could be assured of respect from his fellow citizens, he would be known locally as 'Nelson's man'.
The official advertisements appeared in 1847, asking for sailors who had served in the naval battles of 1793-1840, to send in their written applications for the 'Naval War Medal', applications to be addressed to the Secretary of the Admiralty, Whitehall.
If the old veteran did not, or could not read the advertisements in the London Gazette of 1st and 4th of June 1847, or the newspapers carrying these details, there would be plenty of people who would be only too ready to advise him of the situation, or even assist him with the written application, infact it was considered a patriotic duty to help these old Trafalgar sailors. It is therefore no surprise to find that ex-crew members of *Victory* submitted the highest number of applications to the Secretary of the Admiralty, for the 'Naval War Medal', compared with the surviving crews of other ships in Nelson's victorious fleet.

In my listing of known recipients of the NGS medal, clasp Trafalgar, who served on *Victory* during the battle of 21st October 1805. I could trace but 119 men. I have included within this list, Antonio La Mott and Andrew McDowall, both these names do not appear in *Victory's* Muster Table. Both had their application for service on *Victory* at Trafalgar confirmed and approved by the Admiralty. It could be that they served in 1805 under a different name, or perhaps their application was incorrectly logged by the Admiralty clerk.
Mistakes by the clerks did occur, one such instance was the approving of the NGS medal to Midshipman Robert Smith, who was killed on *Victory* during the battle of Trafalgar and buried at sea on 21st October 1805, ship's casualty ticket number 510. Another strange multiple error, concerns the issuing of four separate NGS medals to the same man, each medal having attached one of his four or maybe five entitled clasps. The recipient who had the chance to wear four NGS medals pinned to his

chest at the same time, was the gallant John Gaze, who served as Master of the Fleet in 1812, under Sir Edward Pellew, (Viscount Exmouth).

The NGS medal clasp Trafalgar, named to James Parker of the *Victory*, is noted as being delivered to his widow in 1849, possibly a case of a man of 68 years of age, who correctly made his application for the medal, but died whilst awaiting its arrival. It is worth noting that had the medal been issued with the wrong or missing clasps, the widow or relative would be entitled to return the medal for additional clasps or corrections, provided death of the recipient had occurred after 1st June 1847.

From papers seen some years ago at the Royal Mint, Tower Hill, it became obvious that a considerable number of very late applications for the Naval General Service Medal and its clasps were accepted by the Admiralty, these late applications were processed and struck by the Mint long after the Admiralty's own closing deadline of May 1851. In many cases these late applications involved additional entitled clasps to previously issued medals, but not always, many late applications for the NGS medal were approved by the Admiralty. All these late medals and clasps were struck by the Mint after 1851, by this time however the original application books were closed, thus these particular awards never appeared in the Admiralty listing of NGS medal clasp applicants, now recorded in the Public Record Office, Kew, under ADM 171/1-7. Many of these late claim clasps are found on medals named to officers, probably because officers had the tenacity and ability to press for their genuine and full entitlement of medal clasps. This could entail endless correspondence with the Secretary to the Admiralty, until finally the officer or man was awarded the correct clasps to his medal, this protracted business may have taken well beyond the May 1851 deadline to complete. Unfortunately the Admiralty 'late claims record book' has long since disapeared. Only the Mint's record that medals and clasps were executed on orders of the Admiralty after 1851, gives the tantalising clue to the existance of these unrecorded awards. I have over the years kept a list of many of these 'late claim' medals and clasps, amongst them are some with the Trafagar clasp.

Could it be possible a sailor from *Victory* was late in submitting his application, or perhaps received his NGS medal with incorrect clasps and had to return the medal for the missing Trafalgar clasp to be added, all this after the May 1851 deadline, perhaps one day we might see surface an additional clasp or medal to the flagship.

THE MISSING GREENWICH MEDALS TO VICTORY

I was struck by the fact that of the twenty six Greenwich Hospital Pensioners who served on *Victory* and were awarded the NGS medal clasp Trafalgar, so far eighteen of these medals have apparently not appeared in collections or museums. It is known when a pensioner died at Greenwich Hospital his medals were often retained by the Hospital. Could it be the Lords Commisioners of the Admiralty used them in silver presentation dishes, in such a way that the medals could not be identified?

In past years all seven parishes located in the North Tyne Valley, Northumberland, and one church in Alston, Cumberland, were under the patronage of the Royal Hospital Greenwich. The Rectors and Vicars of these churches had been at one time Naval Chaplains, since retired from naval service they had been placed by patronage in these parishes. It would seem that the Commissioners of the Admiralty to reinforce their association, presented silver alms dishes to the churches, these alms dishes were made up from medals formerly belonging to pensioners of the Royal Hospital Greenwich. The medals are deeply set into the silver alms dishes, unfortunately the impressed name of the recipient on the edge of the medal remains hidden from sight. As many Trafalgar medals were used as a decorative feature in these six alms dishes plus the large dish at the National Maritime Museum, this might well be where the missing 'Victory' medals have resided for all these years.

Falstone Church. A silver alms dish of twelve and half inches diameter, containing within the two and quarter inch rim, six medals, one with a Trafalgar clasp, the medals are arranged with alternating obverse and reverses showing. An engraved inscription reads "*This Alms Dish inlaid with medals formerly belonging to Pensioners of the Royal Hospital Greenwich is presented to the Church of Falstone by the Lords Commissioners of the Admiralty, A.D. 1891.*"

Simonburn Church. This alms dish is slightly smaller than the Falstone dish, again there are six medals within the design, one NGS having the Trafalgar clasp. The inscription is similar but the church name now reads "Simonburn", it has engraved a later presentation date of 1893.

Greystead Church. This alms dish follows the same pattern and inscription as previous, this time the date is 1894. The dish again has six medals within the design, but includes two NGS medals both with Trafalgar clasps.

Wark Church. The alms dish and inscription similar to the previous examples, this time the engraved date reads 1896. Interestingly this alms dish has five Trafalgar clasp medals out of the six used within the design.

Humshaugh Church. Similar dish, but the inscription reads: "*The inlaid medals formerly belonging to Pensioners of the Royal Hospital, Greenwich, were presented to Humshaugh Church by the Lords Commissioners of the Admiralty, Easter 1909. This Alms dish is the gift of Sarah Emily Taylor, Evelyn Lowry and Mary Lowry.*"
Of the six medals set into the dish, four have the Trafalgar clasp.

Alston Church, Cumberland. This alms dish of six medals has inset four NGS medals with the Trafalgar clasp. The inscription on this dish corresponds to that found on the Falstone alms dish, except that the date of presention is shown as 1896.

National Maritime Museum, Greenwich, held in the museum is a mamouth size silver dish of some twenty six inch diameter, this has an astounding 125 silver naval medals set within its design. All the medals are from deceased pensioners of the Royal Hospital Greenwich. The circular edge of the dish is inset with scores of medal clasps laid end to end to form a decorative pattern, these clasps many of which have Trafalgar upon them, have been taken from the medals that appear set deep within the silver base of the plate. Again it is impossible to identify any names of the recipients.

CREW MEMBERS OF HMS VICTORY WHO HAD THEIR CLAIM APPROVED FOR THE NAVAL GENERAL SERVICE MEDAL, CLASP TRAFALGAR. ADM 171-1

ADAMS William, Quarter Master's Mate. GH 7529.
ANDERSON John (1), AB. T/475
ARTHUR John, LM. 3/26
ASLETT Anthony, AB. GH 8362.   *Ran from Greenwich Naval Hospital on 16 July 1847.*
AUNGER George, ORD. GH 8102.   *With Boulton's medal in pewter & Nelson Testimonial medal.*
        Debenham 1901, Glens November 1936. Douglas-Morris collection RN Museum, Portsmouth.

BAGLAY/BAGLEY James, Pte RM. 5/31.
BALL/BOLL Henry, ORD. 64/5.   *Sotheby February 1975*
BATEMAN John, AB/ORD. Y/491.
BEATSON/BETSON Robert, AB. S/318.
BENNETT Richard, Pte RM. GH 4955.   *Needes June 1940. Oakley July 1953, £6.5.0. Baldwin 1954*
BENTOTE/BENTOLE James, LM. 5/27.
BORTHWICK George, LM. S/354.   *Medal has been Brooched. Seen in Salisbury, July 1982.*
BRASKETT John, AB. O/392.
BROWN/BROWNE George, Lieutenant. 6/7.   *Medal in National Maritime Museum, Greenwich.*
BROWN Jacob, Pte RM. Z/752. GH 3062.
BROWN Joseph, ORD. Y/356. GH 1110.
BROWN Joshua, ORD. GH 7696   *Glens July 1953, lot 63. Re-named medal as "Josh Brown"*
BROWNING William D., Pte RM. O/131
BUCKLEY Conelius, LM. GH 5225.
BURGIN Joseph, ORD. GH 161.
BUTTON Joseph, LM. S/615.   *Glens October 1947 lot 6, sold for £8.10.0.*

CAPPEL Jacob, Pte RM. GH 9146.
CARROLL Cornelius, Boy 2nd class. 5/33   *Christie's November 1986, sold for £1,300.*
CARSLAKE John, Midshipman. 5/28.   *With family in 1990, possibly due for RN Museum.*
CHAMBERS Thomas, Pte RM. X/425
CHAPELL/CHAPPELL Charles, Midshipman/MM. 46/19.   *Glens September 1919, sold for £4.7.6.*
CHAPMAN James, LM. X/121.
CLARKE George, ORD. U/712.
CLARKE William, AB. 6/15
CLAY John, Volunteer, Boy 1st class. 3/27
CLEMENTS Michael, Ship's Corporal. GH 6392.
CONNELL Joseph, ORD. GH 5792.

DOBLE/DOUBLE Robert, Carpenter's Crew. T/538.   *Glens February 1932, £3. Mackenzie June 1934.*
DRUMMOND Robert, AB. 2/39.   *Sotheby June 1977, lot 12.*

EBBS John, Gunner's Mate. S/47.

FEARALL Daniel, Sergeant RM. Q/82.
FELTON John, Midshipman. S/51.
FRENCH George, ORD. GH 5632.

GOBLE Thomas, Master's Mate. 2/36.   *With named Boulton's medal in pewter.*
GRAHAM Thomas, LM. S/234
GREEN Samuel, Pte RM. O/936   *Cheylesmore July 1930. Sotheby December 1990, sold for £2,500.*

HALL William, AB. O/414
HARDING Henry, Pte RM. GH 8893 (or 5893).
HARRISON William, ORD. O/174.
HARTNELL James, Ropemaker. 64/4.
HEATH John, Carpenter's Crew.
HINES James, Pte RM. 5/26   *Admiralty despatched medal 27 June 1849.*
HUNTER John, AB. O/180.   *Hayward List March 1973, £170. Glens July 1976, lot 107.*

JATER Mark, ORD. 46/15.
JOHNS Thomas, AB. S/982.
JOHNSON James (1), Quarter Master's Mate. 70/5.

LAKING/LAYKING Charles, ORD. GH 1644   *Glens April 1964, lot 96, sold for £58.*
LA MOTT Antonio, ORD.   *Not shown on Victory's muster roll under this name.*
          His service on Victory confirmed by Admiralty who granted the NGS medal, clasp Trafalgar.
LANCASTER Henry, Volunteer Boy 1st class. 64/3.   *Glens 19 April 1929, to Newnham collection.*
          Baldwin's November 1975, sold at £975, Peter Dale collection.
LAURIE/LAWRIE Thomas, ORD. S/91
LEVERICK/LEVERICKS Thomas, ORD. O/423.
LYONS John, Midshipman. O/420.

MAINLAND William, AB. O/216.
MANNELL William, Quarter Master's Mate. 9/3.   *Glens Dec. 1923. Glens July 1953, sold for £8.*
          Now in the National Maritime Museum Greenwich.
MANNING John, ORD. O/205.
MARAT Thomas, Supernumary S/92.
MARSH Henry, ORD. O/595.   *Gray Sale May 1920. Sang Sale January 1931. Glens June 1947.*
MARTIN George, AB. S/339.
McBETH Alexander, LM. P/25.
McDOWALL Andrew, Quarter Master's Mate. O/812.   *Not shown on Victory's muster roll under this*
          name. Service on Victory confirmed by Admiralty who granted NGS medal, clasp Trafalgar.
MOSER alias REYNOLDS Peter, AB. Z/972. GH 1695. REYNOLDS on Victory's Muster Roll.
          Glens July 1969. Spink February 1971. Douglas-Morris collection in RN Museum, Portsmouth.
MUNDAY/MONDAY John, ORD. S/221. GH 9845.

NICHOLLS Henry, ORD. O/225.
NIPPER James, AB. 13/21.   *Eaton 1880. Cheylesmore July 1930, lot 617, sold for £7.*
NORVELL/NORVILLE Robert, ORD. O/224.   *Sotheby September. 1978, lot 19, sold for £700.*

PARKER James, ORD. 1/17. ORD on Victory's muster roll, Pte RM on NGS roll.
          James Parker's NGS medal was delivered to his widow on 10th April 1849.
PASCOE/PASCO John, Flag Lieutenant. 2/35.
PEPPETT Charles/James, Boy 2nd class. P/49.   *At Greenwich Hospital as 'Pegley'. GH 7669.*
PILL/PILLE John, AB. Q/296.   *Spink sold medal 2nd May 1962.*
PITNEY Francis, Pte RM. P/959.
PITT George, ORD. Q/628.
POAD James, Midshipman. 2/44.   *Spink June 1986, lot 300, sold at £2,700.*
POLLARD John, Midshipman. 1/50.
POPE William, Boy 1st class. P/431.
PORTER Abraham, Supernumerary. U/674.   *Entered Greenwich Naval Hospital, number not shown.*
POWELL David, Pte RM. Z/932.
POWELL Richard, ORD. 2/5.

RANDEL/RANDALL Thomas, AB. S/107.   *With family. Has named Boulton's medal in pewter.*
REEVES Lewis B. 2nd Lieutenant RM. 7/13.   *Elson February 1963, Lot 11, sold for £185.*
RIVERS William, Midshipman. 5/30.   *Now in the RN Museum, Portsmouth.*
ROBINS Thomas L., Master's Mate. 9/13.
ROOME/ROME John, LM. 29/5. GH 9592.   *Said to have hoisted Nelson's signal. Died 1860.*
ROSS Robert, LM.   *Glens October 1931, Lot 212, sold for £3.17.6.*
ROTELEY/ROATLEY Lewis, 2nd Lieutenant RM. T/712.
ROWE/ROE Michael, AB. S/62.
ROWLEY/ROWLAND Lewis, Pte RM. T/720.

SANDERS/SAUNDERS William, AB. 59/3.   *Glens September 1991, £720. Medal named 'Saunders'.*
SAUNDERS John, Boy 3rd class. 5/29.
SHARMAN/SHERMAN James, ORD. 5/34.   *Sotheby 25 May 1908, lot 85, sold for £1.12.0.*
SHEPPERD/SHEPPARD William, Pte RM.   *Spink unconfirmed medal in 1936. Kingscott 1971.*
SMITH Charles, Carpenter's Crew. Z/253.
SMITH Robert, Midshipman. 64/8.   *Confirmed killed at Trafalgar, 21 October 1805.*
     Against Admiralty regulations this NGS medal was delivered to the Watford family in 1849.
SMITH William (4), AB. X/220.   *Eaton 1880. Cheylesmore July 1930. Glens Sept 1962.*
SMITHSON James, AB. T/756. GH 6556.
SOUTH John, Pte RM. S/320.
SPENCER Samuel, Master's Mate. 5/32.   *Mackenzie 1934, sold for £4/10s. Spink December 1987.*
STEVENS Samuel, LM. 24/14.
STEWART Charles, AB. GH 9346.   *Glens July 1977, Lot 336, sold for £780.*
STRAHAN/STAYHAM/STRAWN Thomas, LM. Q/9.   *Greenwich Hospital as 'Stracham' GH 6936.*
STYLES/STILES Henry, LM. GH 5376.   *Massie September 1961, Lot 55, sold for £42.*
SUTHERLAND James, ORD. T/756.
SYMONS William H., Master's Mate. 3/39.   *Spink September 1986 Lot 211, sold for £3,100.*

TARRANT/TERRANT William, Quarter Gunner 70/4.   *Noted with family in June 1977.*
TART John, ORD. O/613. Glens May 1937.   *Author's collection 1993.*
THOMPSON William (4), ORD. 70/3.   *MacDougall June 1917. Glens Jan. 1931. Glens June 1952.*
     Now in the National Maritime Museum Greenwich.
TOMBLESON/TOMLINSON Thomas, Carpenter's Crew. 1/2.   *With Boulton's medal in pewter.*
     Whitaker 1890. Christie's July 1983.
TUCK John, Pte RM. T/377.

WALKER/ROBERTSON James, Midshipman. 81/2.   *Changed his name to James Robertson Walker.*
     on his marriage in 1824. NGS medal named to 'James Robertson'.
WARD Edward, Pte RM. P/267.
WARD George, Supernumerary. T/450.   *Sotheby November 1984, lot 4, sold for £935.*
WEST James (1), LM. GH 9239.   *Ran from Greenwich Naval Hospital on 25 July 1848.*
WESTPHAL George A., Midshipman. 24/15.   *Glens December 1954, sold for £44. Hayward 1980.*
WISE Edward, AB. 30/18.
WIZEN/WIZZEN George, Pte RM. 2/4.

The spelling of the recipient's name shown on this roll, is that appearing on his written application submitted to the Secretary of the Admiralty, when claiming for the "Naval War Medal". This may differ from the spelling entered in Victory's Muster Table. Names were often given phonetically, sometimes in a heavy brogue or dialect, causing variations to the name entered by the ship's clerk.

In the above roll, the first number appearing after the recipient's rank, is that used by the Admiralty clerks when identifying and checking medal claims during the period 1847-49.
The number preceded by the letters "GH" refers to the entrance number of those sailors accepted by Greenwich Naval Hospital.

THE NAVAL GENERAL SERVICE MEDAL 1793-1840

Obverse

Reverse

MR. BOULTON'S TRAFALGAR MEDAL 1805

Obverse

Reverse

MR. DAVISON'S TRAFALGAR MEDAL 1805

Obverse

Reverse

PRIVATELY AWARDED MEDALS FOR TRAFALGAR

It would not complete the story of the men of *HMS Victory* and the rewards for Trafalgar, if the two unofficial medals issued by Mr. Boulton and Mr. Davison were not included. These medals after all were the first tangible tokens of esteem bestowed upon junior officers and men of the lower deck, for their part in the Battle of Trafalgar. Admirals and Captains would receive the appropriate Naval Gold Medals to confirm their service at Trafalgar. But it would take until 1848, for those men who survived the years, to be able to claim for the '*Naval War Medal*', and finally receive recognition by way of a medal, for their part in making Britain ruler of the waves.

Mr. Boulton's Trafalgar Medal. This 48mm medal was produced at Mr. Boulton's personal expense, after gaining official permission these privately struck medals were presented to the survivors of the Battle of Trafalgar. Medals were produced in gold, silver and pewter. Those found in bronze and in bronze-gilt should be considered as proof display pieces only. The type of metal used was to reflect the rank and status of the recipient. In general it was given in silver to officers and pewter to ratings. Sometimes the medal is found encased within a silver or copper band and glazed, from this band a swivel suspender ring was attached, this circular collar unfortunately hides the impressed wording found around the edge of the medal, which reads: FROM M. BOULTON TO THE HEROES OF TRAFALGAR. The obverse shows a well executed bust of Nelson in Admirals uniform, surrounded by his title, reverse the historic signal: ENGLAND EXPECTS EVERY MAN WILL DO HIS DUTY, this encircles a scene of the battle, below in two lines TRAFALGAR OCT. 21. 1805. On those medals without the circular silver or copper band, a hole was drilled in the medal approximately above the head of Lord Nelson and a suspender ring was attached. The ribbon that passed through this ring was dark blue, known at that time as the "Trafalgar ribbon". The medal was issued un-named, but occasionally the recipient had the blank area on the reverse field of the medal privately engraved with his name and sometimes the ship he served on.

The author of these medals of patriotic esteem and regard, was Mr. Matthew Boulton, of Soho Mint, Birmingham, a wealthy manufacturer. He commissioned the designer C. H. Kuchler to produce a fitting medallic tribute to bestow upon those men who had fought at Trafalgar, Britain's greatest naval victory. It should be remembered that in 1806, the only medals awarded so far for Trafalgar were the Naval Large Gold Medal presented to Admirals, and the Naval Small Gold Medal awarded to Captains. In two cases Naval Small Gold Medals were awarded to Lieutenants who were acting as Captains at Trafalgar.

In November 1837, a Lieutenant who had served as a Midshipman on *Achille* at Trafalgar, submitted a letter to The Lords Commissioners of the Admiralty with regard to the wearing of his silver Boulton's Trafalgar medal, the only medal this officer had been awarded to confirm his part in the battle of 21st October 1805. This letter now in the Public Records Office, Kew, under ref: (ADM1/2915. LIEUT G99), is set out below.

Sir, I respectfully beg to state that on the 21st October 1805, I had the honour of serving in *HMS Achille* in the Battle of Trafalgar, and that with other officers, I received through the Government as a mark of distinction in commemoration of that great event a Silver Medal: having frequently seen this medal worn by persons to whom it had been presented, suspended by the Trafalgar ribbon, and it being customary for officers and men of the Army to wear Medals, which had been granted to them on account of any great military exploit. I take the liberty, Sir, most respectfully to request you will do me the favour to inform me whether The Lords Commissioners of the Admiralty would object to my wearing my Medal or not. A certificate from the late Admiral Sir Richard King, who was my Captain in the Battle is enclosed; and with the utmost deference begging Their Lordship's sanction. (*Signed*) J. C. Gill, Lieutenant.

A reply from the Admiralty dated 27 November 1837, stated briefly: 'Their Lordships cannot sanction the wearing of a private Medal.'

It is interesting that the letter confirms that the Government had sanctioned the distribution of this privately issued Boulton's medal. Also the writer describes a ribbon known at that time as the 'Trafalgar ribbon,' was used to suspend this same medal. As only old snippets of dark blue ribbon have been seen over the years with these medals, it can be assumed this must be the 'Trafalgar ribbon' mentioned. Another point is the fact that he as a Midshipman received the silver Boulton's medal.

Mr. Davison's Trafalgar Medal. This 54mm medal in pewter was issued privately by Mr. Alexander Davison, Nelson's prize-agent. About 1,000 were was struck to be awarded to the ratings of *HMS Victory*, who had served so gallantly at the Battle of Trafalgar. This pewter medal is often found encircled by a copper band, some examples have been noted with a silver band, from this additional collar a ring had been attached to act as a suspender for the dark blue ribbon, the same ribbon as used on Boulton's Trafalgar medal.

The designer was a Mr. Halliday, he crammed both obverse and reverse of the medal with a multitude of words and dates, obverse with the legend partly in Latin, shows a shield surmounted by a very small bust of Lord Nelson, the reverse central design shows *Victory* with her sails reefed. This medal was issued un-named, but sometimes the medal is found privately engraved on the reverse with the recipient's details.

This was not Mr. Davison's first venture into producing and distributing privately struck medals at his own expense, as a mark of his regard for the patriotic endeavours of Nelson's victorious fleet at the Battle of the Nile, August 1798, Mr. Davison had stuck and distributed to all officers and men present at the battle, medals in gold, silver, bronze-gilt and bronze.

Ships under the command of Lord Nelson at Trafalgar

21 October 1805

Guns

104	VICTORY Vice-Admiral Lord Nelson, K.B. Captain Thomas Masterman Hardy	*57 killed, 75 wounded*
100	ROYAL SOVEREIGN Vice-Admiral C. Collingwood. Captain Edward Rotheram	*47 killed, 94 wounded*
100	BRITANNIA Rear-Admiral the Earl of Northesk. Captain Charles Bullen	*10 killed, 42 wounded*
98	TEMERAIRE Captain Eliab Harvey.	*47 killed, 76 wounded*
98	NEPTUNE Captain Thomas Francis Fremantle.	*10 killed, 34 wounded*
98	DREADNOUGHT Captain John Conn.	*7 killed, 26 wounded*
98	PRINCE Captain Richard Grindall.	*Casualties notified late*
80	TONNANT Captain Charles Tyler.	*26 killed, 50 wounded*
74	BELLEISLE Captain William Hargood.	*33 killed, 93 wounded*
74	REVENGE Captain Robert Moorsom.	*28 killed, 51 wounded*
74	SPARTIATE Captain Sir Francis Laforey, Bart.	*3 killed, 19 wounded*
74	MARS Captain George Duff. *Killed in Action.*	*29 killed, 69 wounded*
74	DEFIANCE Captain Philip Charles Durham.	*17 killed, 53 wounded*
74	MINOTAUR Captain Charles John Moore Mansfield	*3 killed, 22 wounded*
74	CONQUEROR Captain Israel Pellew.	*3 killed, 9 wounded*
74	ACHILLE Captain Sir Richard King, Bart.	*3 killed, 59 wounded*
74	COLOSSUS Captain James Nicoll Morris.	*40 killed, 160 wounded*
74	DEFENCE Captain George Johnstone Hope.	*7 killed, 29 wounded*
74	LEVIATHAN Captain Henry William Bayntun.	*4 killed, 22 wounded*
74	BELLEROPHON Captain John Cooke. *Killed in Action.*	*27 killed, 123 wounded*
74	ORION Captain Edward Codrington.	*1 killed, 23 wounded*
74	SWIFTSURE Captain William George Rutherford.	*9 killed, 8 wounded*
74	AJAX Lieutenant John Pilfold, (Acting Captain).	*2 killed, 9 wounded*
74	THUNDERER Lieutenant John Stockham, (Act. Captain).	*4 killed, 12 wounded*
64	POLYPHEMUS Captain Robert Redmill.	*2 killed, 4 wounded*
64	AFRICA Captain Henry Digby.	*18 killed, 44 wounded*
64	AGAMEMNON Captain Sir Edward Berry, Kt.	*2 killed, 7 wounded*
36	EURYALUS, Frigate Captain the Hon. Henry Blackwood.	
36	PHOEBE, Frigate Captain the Hon. Thomas Bladen Capel.	
36	NAIAD, Frigate Captain Thomas Dundas.	
36	SIRIUS, Frigate Captain William Prowse.	
10	PICKLE, Schooner Lieutenant John Richard Lapenotiere.	
8	ENTREPRENANTE, Cutter Lieutenant Robert Benjamin Young.	

The figures showing numbers of killed and wounded for each ship are those supplied by surgeons to their Captains immediately after the battle for transmission to Vice-Admiral Lord Collingwood. It was neccessary to inform the Admiralty urgently of the damage and casualties sustained by the fleet during the battle. Those dangerously injured men who were to die of their wounds later, appeared on the Captain's initial report as severely wounded. The report could not take into account those men with slight wounds who did not present themselves to the surgeons.

The Combined French and Spanish fleet at Trafalgar

French Fleet

80	BUCENTAURE	Vice-Admiral Villeneuve.	*197 killed, 85 wounded*
		Captain Jean-Jacques Magendie	
80	FORMIDABLE	Rear-Admiral Dumanoir-le-Pelley.	*22 killed, 45 wounded*
		Captain Jean-Marie Letellier	
80	NEPTUNE	Commodore Esprit-Tranquille Maistral.	*15 killed, 39 wounded*
80	INDOMPTABLE	Commodore Jean-Joseph Hubert.	*Two thirds of the crew drowned*
74	ALGESIRAS	Rear-Admiral Charles Magon.	*77 killed, 142 wounded*
		Captain Gabriel-Auguste Brouard	
74	PLUTON	Commodore Julian-Marie Cosmao Kerjulien.	*60 killed, 132 wounded*
74	MONT BLANC	Commodore Guill-Jean-Noel la Villegris.	*20 killed, 20 wounded*
74	INTREPIDE	Commodore Louis-Antoine-Cyprien Infornet.	*Half of the crew perished*
74	SWIFTSURE	Captain L'Hospitalier-Villemadrin.	*68 killed, 123 wounded*
74	AIGLE	Captain Pierre-Paul Gourrege.	*Two thirds of the crew lost*
74	SCIPION	Captain Charles Berenger.	*17 killed, 22 wounded*
74	DUGUAY TROUIN	Captain Claude Touffet.	*12 killed, 24 wounded*
74	BERWICK	Captain Jean-Gilles Filhol-Camas.	*Only a handful survived the wreck*
74	ARGONAUTA	Captain Jacques Epron.	*55 killed, 137 wounded*
74	ACHILLE	Captain Gabriel Denieport.	*480 casualties*
74	REDOUTABLE	Captain Jean-Jacques-Etienne Lucas.	*490 killed, 81 wounded*
74	FOUGUEUX	Captain Louis-Alexis Beaudouin.	*546 casualties*
74	HEROS	Captain Jean-Bap-Jos-Remi Poulain.	*12 killed, 26 wounded*

Also engaged but casualties not identified for the frigates: CONELIE, HERMIONE, HORTENSE, RHIN, THEMIS, also no casualties known for the brigs FURET and ARGUS.

Spanish Fleet

130	SANTISSIMA TRINIDAD	Rear-Admiral Don Hidalgo Cisneros.	*216 killed, 116 wounded*
		Commodore Don Francisco de Uriarte	
112	PRINCIPE de ASTURIAS	Admiral Don Frederico Gravina.	*54 killed, 109 wounded*
		Rear-Admiral Don Antonio Escano	
112	SANTA ANA	Vice-Admiral Don Ign. Maria de Alava.	*104 killed, 137 wounded*
		Captain Don Josef Gardoqui	
100	RAYO	Commodore Don Enrique Macdonel.	*4 killed, 14 wounded*
80	NEPTUNO	Commodore Don Cayetano Valdes.	*38 killed, 35 wounded*
80	ARGONAUTA	Commodore Don Antonio Parejas.	*103 killed, 202 wounded*
74	BAHAMA	Captain Don Dionisio Galiano.	*75 killed, 66 wounded*
74	MONTAÑES	Captain Don Josef Salzedo.	*20 killed, 29 wounded*
74	SAN AGUSTIN	Captain Don Felipe Xado Cagigal.	*184 killed, 201 wounded*
74	SAN ILDEFONSO	Captain Don Josef Bargas.	*36 killed, 129 wounded*
74	SAN JUAN NEPOMUCENO	Captain Don Cosme Churruca.	*103 killed, 151 wounded*
74	MONARCA	Captain Don Teodoro Argumosa.	*101 killed, 154 wounded*
74	SAN FRANCISCO de ASIS	Captain Don Luis de Flores.	*5 killed, 12 wounded*
74	SAN JUSTO	Captain Don Miguel Gaston.	*7 wounded*
64	SAN LEANDRO	Captain Don Josef Quevedo.	*8 killed, 22 wounded*

LIST OF PRISONERS ON BOARD VICTORY

Included are 40 prisoners taken during the Battle of Trafalgar. Three of these men swam to the *Victory* and were taken on board during the action. All of these prisoners were entered in the muster book for victuals, at the reduced rate of two thirds.

Prisoners were discharged on 29th October 1805 at Gibraltar Bay, with the excepton of Captain Villemadrin of the French ship *Swiftsure*, he remained on *Victory* until the 31st of October, possibly being entertained until arrangements could be made for his exchange and return to France.

1. Antonie MONTMERALLA. Swam to *Victory*, on board during battle of 21 October.
2. Jessemaxa ALZORES. Swam to *Victory*, on board during battle of 21 October.
3. Joseca HEICO. Swam to *Victory*, on board during battle of 21 October.
4. Andw. DUPUIS. Picked up by the Schooner *Pickle*, saved from *Achille*. Arrived 23 October .
5. Jos GABARAE. On board 23 October.
6. John GALLIER. On board 23 October.
7. Jean ROEA. On board 23 October.
8. Louis DELORISH. On board 23 October.
9. Francois LUGERATE. On board 23 October.
10. Jos POGERO. On board 23 October.
11. John GILLETT. On board 23 October.
12. Mitchell FERRAS. On board 23 October.
13. Charles GILMATE. On board 23 October.
14. Jos AVONGE. On board 23 October.
15. Louis GODDIN. On board 23 October.
16. Jno MAZZOD. On board 23 October.
17. Eli ALLAV. On board 23 October.
18. Gillier Le QUARTE. On board 23 October.
19. John AUCHALL. On board 23 October.
20. Dennis COCKADE. On board 23 October.
21. Louis BELVARE. Picked up by Schooner Pickle from *Achille*. Arrived 23 October
22. John BERGI. On board 23 October.
23. Jean Briar. On board 23 October.
24. Martin MARSEILLES. On board 23 October.
25. Antonie JAFFIER On board 23 October.
26. Victor Le CROIS. On board 23 October.
27. Joseph RICAR. On board 23 October.
28. Phelix CAVIER. On board 23 October.
29. Jervaise ROSSHERON. On board 23 October.
30. Fredk. NALLUST. On board 23 October.
31. Jarvis SIRLLOY. On board 23 October.
32. Maxima VOEM. On board 23 October.
33. Antonie JAMARD. On board 23 October.
34. Joseph CHARBIER. On board 23 October.
35. Jemari CONGRI. On board 23 October.
36. Etemiu SEYROS. On board 23 October.
37. Romant BALVIREE. On board 23 October.
38. Antonie MARTIN. On board 23 October.
39. Judith COMADU. On board 23 October.
40. L'Hospitalier-VILLEMADRIN, Captain of the French ship *Swiftsure*, on board *Victory* 31 October

These forty names were entered in the muster for victuals, and noted by Walter Burke the purser and confirmed by Captain Hardy's signature. In the margin of the Muster Table the note: "*Discharged 29 October 1805 Cartel Gibraltar Bay.*"

BIOGRAPHICAL NOTES ON SOME CREW MEMBERS OF VICTORY

ADAIR Charles William, Captain RM. Born 1776 at Loughanmore, Dunadry, County Antrim. The son of Lieutenant-Colonel Benjamin Adair, R.M., his mother Susannah was the sister of Captain William Prowse who commanded *Sirius* at Trafalgar.
Charles Wiliam Adair joined the Royal Marines as a 2nd Lieutenant in 1782, promoted Lieutenant 1793. He was at the capture of the Cape in 1795. Appointed Captain in 1800. On the commissioning of *Victory* at Chatham April 1803, Adair was the senior Marine officer. At Trafalgar this gallant officer leading a party of marines successfully repelled borderers from the *Redoutable*. During this action he was positioned on a gangway close alongside the French ship, when a musket ball struck him fatally in the neck. In this desperate affair against borderers *Victory* had eighteen men killed and twenty injured.

ATKINSON Thomas, Master. Born 1768. Appointed Master, R.N. in 1795. Served as Master of the *Theseus* at Teneriffe in 1797. Saw service at the Battle of the Nile 1798. Commanded a boat at the siege of Acre 1799 where he was wounded. Served as Master for Nelson on board *Elephant* at Copenhagen in 1801. Nelson held Atkinson in great esteem and was godfather to one of his sons, the son carried the name Horatio Nelson Atkinson. At Trafalgar as Master of *Victory* he had the flagship placed against the enemy line perfectly as ordered. At Nelson's funeral he attended the coffin with the officers of *Victory*. Thomas Atkinson served as 1st Master Attendant at Portsmouth Dockyard from 1823 until his death at the age of 69 years in June 1836. He was buried at a church near Portsmouth.

AUNGER George, ORD. Born 1782 at Exeter. In May 1799 George Aunger joined The Exeter Regiment of Volunteers as a Private. He was a good marksman and in October 1800 was awarded a silver medal for being the "Second Best Shot" in 1st Company. In May 1803 he volunteered for the Royal Navy and within days was mustered on board *Victory*. He came through the Trafalgar action unscathed and was awarded Mr Boulton's Trafalgar medal. Served in the navy for a further five years. In November 1843 he was accepted at Greenwich Naval Hospital. In 1844 he received the Nelson Testimonial medal and in 1848 was awarded the Naval General Service Medal clasp Trafalgar. George Aunger died September 1859.

BAILEY Thomas, Gunner's Mate. Born 1773. During the Battle of Trafalgar, Thomas Bailey was serving the guns when a shot came through and struck a young Midshipman named William Rivers, smashing his leg just below the knee. Bailey who knew the lad well, he was the son of the ship's Gunner Mr. Rivers, gently picked up the Midshipman and carried him down the stairway to the cockpit, ready for the surgeon's attention. Returning to the guns, he saw Nelson approaching who ordered him to aim his gun at the foreriggings of the *Redoubtable,* which he did. This was Nelson's last order before he was struck down. Thomas Bailey entered the Greenwich Naval Hospital in 1832

BARTON Robert Cutts, Midshipman. Born 1785 in Pembrokeshire. Joined *Victory* on the 31st July 1803. After Trafalgar his gallantry was rewarded by promotion to Lieutenant in 1806. He further distinguished himself on 31st October/1st November 1809, during a spirited action in the boats of the frigate *Apollo,* under heavy fire from the battery of Castle of Rosas, he was involved with other boats in the successfull cutting out of a convoy of eleven French ships, burning some and capturing others. Promoted Commander in 1819. He died at Bideford, Devon in 1827.

BEATTY William, Surgeon. Born 1773 at St Andrews, Scotland. Appointed Royal Naval Surgeon 1793. Saw considerabl active service prior to joining *Victory* from the Mediterranean on 31st December 1804. Beatty attended Nelson as he laid dying in the cockpit, the most illustrious patient that any naval surgeon has ever attended. The 21st of October 1805 was to change Beatty's life and elevate his career. Later Beatty published in 1807 his graphic account of Nelson's death, under the title *Authentic Narrative of the Death of Lord Nelson*. After Trafalgar in 1806, he was appointed Physician to the Fleet, serving under Admiral Sir John Jervis. Honoured with M.D. of St. Andrews 1817. Became a Licentiate of the College of Physicians 1817. F.R.S., 1818. In 1822 he became Physician of Greenwich Naval Hospital. Knighted in 1831. He died at Portman Square, London in 1842.

BLIGH George Miller, Lieutenant. Born 1784 at Alverstoke, Portsmouth. Son of Admiral Sir Richard Rodney Bligh. This officer entered the Royal Navy in 1794 as a ten year old Midshipman. In November of the same year he was taken prisoner when the 74-gun *Alexander*, commanded by his father, was captured off the coast of Sicily. In March 1795 the crew were released by the French and returned to England. Bligh was promoted to Lieutenant in 1801. Joined *Victory* as senior Lieutenant when she was commissioned in 1803. At Trafalgar he was severly wounded when struck in the head by a French musket ball. Was one of the supporter to the bearer of the Banner of Emblems at Nelson's funeral. Promoted Commander in 1806. Captain of the sloop *Pylades* at the capture of a privateer *Grand Napoleon* in 1808. Commanded the sloop *Acorn* on guard duties at Lissa. Died in 1834 at Portsmouth and is buried at Alverstoke.

BROWNE/BROWN George, Lieutenant. Born in 1784 at Bridgewater, Somerset. Entered the Royal Navy in 1797 as a Midshipman. Joined *Victory* from *Amphion* on 31st July 1803, promoted Master's Mate in September 1803, promoted Signal Lieutenant August 1804. At Trafalgar was present and assisted as the signal was hoisted: "England expects that every man will do his duty". Browne was directed to take charge of the fore guns on the middle deck during the action. At Nelson's funeral he, with other lieutenants of the *Victory*, carried the bannerol of lineage. In 1806 he joined on *Ocean* as Flag Lieutenant under Admiral Lord Collingwood. When the Admiral removed to the *Ville de Paris*, Browne went with him. Admiral Lord Collingwood died in March 1809 whilst serving in the Mediterranean, Lieutenant Browne accompanied the Admirals remains back to England, and was promoted Commander on his return. With appointments difficult to obtain Browne entered to study law at the Inner Temple, being called to the bar in 1821. JP for Somerset and Bridgewater. Retired Captain September 1840. Died 1856.

BULKELEY Richard, Midshipman. Born 1787. Although his family came from the village of Pencombe, Bromyard near Hereford, the Midshipman had entered in the ship's muster his home as America. Bulkeley joined *Victory* in the Mediterranean from the *Amphion* in July 1803. He was slightly wounded at Trafalgar, for his gallantry promoted Lieutenent in 1806. When *Victory* reached England a considerable number of the crew were drafted to the 98-gun *Ocean*, the flagship of Admiral Lord Collingwood, Bulkeley was one of the officers who joined this ship. He left the Royal Navy in 1810.

BURGIN Joseph, ORD/Poulter. Born 1778 in Bishop's Stortford. He joined the Royal Navy under the name of Joseph Coxhead, in February 1798, aged 20 years. His first ship was *Vanguard*, he was initially rated as Landsman then promoted to Ordinary Seaman. As ORD he served on Nelson's flagship *Vanguard* at the Battle of the Nile 1798. His next ship was *Aurora* which he joined in March 1800, he was discharged from her in April 1802 when the fragile peace of Amiens broke out. When hostilities once more commenced, Burgin again joined the Royal Navy in April 1803, and received a bounty of £2 as a volunteer. He joined *Victory* on 11th May 1803, entered in the Muster Table as Joseph Burgin alias Coxhead, rated as ORD/Poulter. At Trafalgar he was stationed on the 13th gun on the middle deck, he was dangerously wounded with his leg shattered by round shot, taken to the cockpit where the surgeon amputated his left leg high up from his thigh. He was one of the badly wounded taken to the Naval Hospital Gibraltar, he was returned home on the *Sussex*. Burgin was discharged as "Invalided" from *Sussex* when she reached England on 18 January 1806. Entered as a patient at Greenwich Hospital on 7th April 1806, he was resident there for an amazing fifty-six years and died at Greenwich Hospital in July 1862.

BURKE Walter, Purser. Born in 1738, it is said he came from an Irish family related to the political philosopher Edmund Burke. He was the oldest crew member to serve on *Victory* at Tafalgar, being 67 at the time of the action. Burke who had been on deck during the thick of the action, had been noticed by Nelson who remarked "Mr. Burke , I expect every man to be upon his station," as the purser's battle station was the cockpit, he immediately removed himself there. When the wounded Nelson was carried down into the cockpit, Burke like the father figure he was, straight away comforted the injured Admiral by supporting the weight of the frail body off the wound with a pillow. Burke stayed with Nelson until the very end. He died at Rochester, Kent in 1815 at the age of 77 years, having survived two of his sons. His eldest son Captain Henry Burke was lost in the *Seagull* in 1805, another son Lieutenant Walter Burke was killed whilst cutting out a French corvette in 1801.

CARSLAKE John/William, Midshipman. Born 1785 in Colyton, Devon. Carslake entered the Royal Navy in 1799 at the age of thirteen as a Boy 1st class. He joined the *Victory* at Chatham in 1803 as a Midshipman. He came to the attention of Captain Hardy, when in May 1804, he discovered and sucessfully fought a fire in the cockpit. He was promoted to Lieutenant immediately after Trafalgar. His courage once more came to note when he rescued a First Lieutenant and a seaman from heavy seas in the English Channel, without hesitation he dived overboard and saved their lives. For this heroic act he was promoted First Lieutenant of the *Prosperine*. In 1809 while off Toulon the *Prosperine* was involved in a stiff fight with two French frigates, unfortunately overwhelmed the crew were taken prisoner. Carslake spent five years as a prisoner, he was incarcerated at Verdun, a citadel being situated over 200 miles from any sea port, setting a real problem for any potential escaper. He was finally released in 1814, as the war drew to a close. Retired as commander in 1852. John Carslake served as Justice of the Peace for Devon. He died at Clifton in 1865.

CARY Henry, Midshipman. Born in 1785 at Portarlington, Ireland. Entered the Royal Navy in 1799 aged fourteen, as a Boy 1st class. Later as a Midshipman he survived the wreck of the *Resistance* when she sank off Cape St. Vincent in May 1803. Joined *Victory* in June 1803. He was one of the group of young Midshipmen who were assembled before the battle and told how rewards flowed from dedication and bravery in action. For his service at Trafalgar Cary was promoted to Master's Mate in November

1805. When the *Victory* was paid off January 1806, Cary joined *Ocean*, the flagship of Admiral Lord Collingwood. Promoted Lieutenant in 1807, he joined *Inflexible* and saw service at Copenhagen 1807, where he served with distinction on shore as a Brigade Major. In the boats of *Kent* he was involved in destroying a convoy sheltering under the protection of the batteries in the Mole of Palamos. In 1813 he gained a shore job in Ireland being employed at the Kerryhead Signal Station, Ballyheige Bay. Cary returned to a sea appointment as First Lieutenant to the *Cyrus* in 1816, with this appointment completed he left the Royal Navy to command a Post Office hired vessel from 1820 until 1834. Retired as Commander in 1843. Died 1847.

CHAPPELL Charles, Master's Mate (Supernumary). Born 1784. Chappell entered the Royal Navy in 1798. He joined the 18-gun *Seagull* as an AB, promoted Midshipman in 1799 then Master's Mate, all these rank progressions on the same ship. From June 1803 he served on the 80-gun *Foudroyant*, followed by service on the 14-gun sloop *Childers*, where he was noted for the capture of a French prize. On 9th October 1805, he joined *Victory* with the rank of Master's Mate. At Trafalgar although he did not figure on the official list of wounded, possibly because he never presented himself to any of the surgeons, he was noted as being wounded on the face. In 1807 he served in the boats of *Chiffonne* during a cutting out affair with a Spanish brig. Promoted Lieutenant 1808. Served in various stations and retired as Commander in 1845. Died 1865.

CHASEMAN William, Master's Mate. Born 1782 in Plymouth. Entered service in 1794 and became a Midshipman in 1799, served on *Amethyst* and was involved in the capture of three privateers plus a French frigate and corvette in 1801. His gallantry at Trafalgar gained him immediate promotion to Lieutenant. His bravery was once again noted when in 1808 serving on *Kent*, he took a party of men under heavy fire and landed at the Italian port of Noli, he captured and spiked the town gun prior to the capture of a convoy of vessels, secured by ropes to the shore, he successfully brought out ten heavily laden coasters. For this action he was mentioned in despatches. Whilst Lieutenant on *Crescent* he captured an American privateer off Newfound in 1814. Commander 1821. Died 1828.

COLLINGWOOD Edward Francis, Midshipman. Born 1785 at Milford, Pembrokeshire. The only son of Francis Collingwood of Greenwich. He entered service on the *Agamemnon* in 1799. In September 1805 he joined *Victory*, rated on the muster as AB, but infact served as Midshipman. During the Battle of Trafalgar it was claimed Collingwood in company with Midshipman Pollard, were both responsible for avenging Nelson's death, by shooting the French marksman responsible. Lieutenant 1806. Served on *Pallas* at destruction of five French men-of-war in 1809. Collingwood was in the ill fated Walcheren expedition of 1809. In later years he was in command of Kite, revenue cutter on the coast of Ireland, 1820-23, whilst carrying out the duties of this command Edward Collingwood was twice wounded. Commander 1828. Died at Tralee, Ireland in 1835, aged 50 years

FELTON John, Midshipman. Born 1784 in Hackney, London. As a Midshipman he served at Copenhagen 1801 on board *Bellona*, this was to be his baptismal of fire, in the engagement no less than eight of the ship's officers were casualties. Joined *Victory* in September 1805, his services at Trafalgar gained him promotion to Lieutenant in 1806. Resigned his commission in 1810. He claimed his NGS medal in 1847, with clasps Copenhagen and Trafalgar.

FRENCH James, AB. Born 1783 at Harwich, Essex. French in 1802 was crew on an East Indiaman returning from China. The merchant ship was boarded by a party from the 64-gun *Utrecht*, they were looking for men to press, unfortunately James French was one of those taken by the press gang to serve the Royal Navy. The *Utrecht* being in need of urgent repairs had to return to England. At Chatham in company with the other members of the East Indiaman, French was transferred to the *Victory*. During the battle of Trafalgar he was one of those whose shared the task of loading one of the 32-pounders, the gun team consisted of seven men, including an Irishman who had been many times in action, it was he who took up the initial loading which was a most strenuous job, after a while it was the turn of French. Some years later James French wrote of his experiences and noted: "Our brave Hibernian now plucked up spirits to load the gun for about ten minutes, the exception of which I had to load the gun the whole of the action, which it was every man's duty to relieve each other here. I saw them fall on the right and on the left whilst I myself was preserved. I was worn out with fatigue." He goes on to say at the close of the fighting he fell into a deep sleep, missing the wine being served to the lower deck after the action. His mentions rather bitterly that when the *Victory* reached England, "Not one hour's liberty on shore but, sent to sea. Immediately we proceeded to Portsmouth to convoy the East India Fleet out past the Madeira Island."

GOBLE Thomas, Master's Mate. Born 1782 at Arundel, Sussex. The son of James Holmes Goble, Major in the Sussex Yeomanry Horse Artillery. Joined *Victory* on 5th of October 1805, as an AB, on 13th October he was promoted to Master's Mate and served as Secretary to Captain Hardy. On the death of Mr. Scott, Lord Nelson's Secretary, Thomas Goble acted as Secretary to the Fleet. The

Muster Table show him as Clerk as from 29th October 1805. Appointed Purser in 1806. Retired in 1825. Died 1869 and is buried at Porchester, Hants.

GREEN James, Midshipman/Master's Mate. Born 1783 at Attlebridge, Norfolk. Joined *Victory* as a Midshipman from the *Canopus* on the 3rd of April 1805. On the 18th of April he was promoted to Master's Mate. His actions at Trafalgar gained him a further promotion this time to Lieutenant in 1806. Last entry in the Navy List for James Green is found in 1812.

GRINDALL Festing Horatio, Midshipman. Born 1787 at Weymouth. Son of Richard Grindall, Captain of the *Prince* at the Battle of Trafalgar and later Vice-Admiral, K.C.B. In July 1803, Festing Horatio Grindall joined *Victory* from the *Amphion* which had recently arrived from England. He did not gain immediate promotion after the battle, but was promoted Lieutenant in 1809. He died in 1812. Grindall joined *Victory* on 31 July 1803, the same day as Lord Nelson and Captain Hardy.

HARDY Thomas Masterman, Captain. Born 1769 at Portisham, Dorset. Educated at Crewkerne and Milton Abbas. Midshipman in *Amphitrite* 1793. Promoted Lieutenant 1793. In the *Minerve* at the Battle of St. Vincent 1797. Commanded the *Mutine* at the Battle of the Nile 1798, for this service promoted Captain 1798. Served in the *Foudroyant* under Nelson off Naples and Sicily. With Nelson at Copenhagen 1801. As the Admiral's Flag-Captain at Trafalgar, he was a witness to Nelson's last will. Was standing beside Nelson when he was mortally wounded. Hardy in the thick of the battle did not hesitate to make several visits to the cockpit to give Nelson comfort and inform him how well the battle was going. The Surgeon William Beatty later described in his narative the sad drama that unfolded in the cockpit: On the second visit, Hardy took Nelson's hand in his and congratulated the dying hero on his brilliant victory, telling him that possibly fourteen or fifteen prizes had been taken. Nelson near to death replied *"That is well, but I had bargained for twenty."* Knowing his friend's life was fast moving to its close, Captain Hardy knelt down and kissed his Lordship on the cheek, Nelson looking up at Hardy said,*"Now I am satisfied. Thank God I have done my duty."* The close bond between the two men had been forged over the previous seven years, had Hardy lived to claim his NGS medal it would have held clasps for the three fleet victories gained by Lord Nelson: NILE, COPENHAGEN and TRAFALGAR, and of course the earlier clasp St Vincent, the fleet victory of Admiral Jervis. For his part in the great victory Hardy was created a baronet, received the Naval small gold medal and the thanks of Parliament. Was presented with a silver vase from the Patriotic Fund and bestowed with a City of London presentation sword. After Trafalgar, Hardy's appointments and rewards were: Commander-in-Chief at Lisbon 1809-12. Commander of a squadron on the North American Station 1812-13. K.C.B. 1815. Commander-in-Chief South American Station 1819-24. Colonel Royal Marines 1821. Rear-Admiral 1825. First Sea Lord of Admiralty 1830-34. G.C.B. 1831. Governor of Greenwhich Hospital 1834. Elder Brother Trinity House 1837. He died in 1839 and was buried at Greenwich Hospital.

HARRINGTON Daniel, Midshipman. Born in 1776 at Waterford, Ireland. Joined *Victory* from the *Donegal* on the 3rd of August 1805. For his gallant service during the Battle of Trafalgar, Harrington was promoted Lieutenant. In November 1805 he joined *Queen*, flagship of Admiral Lord Collingwood. In 1807 as Lieutenant on board *Standard* he was wounded during an expedition to force the Dardenelles. Died at Dieppe, France in 1837

HILLS Alexander, Lieutenant. Born 1780 at Bedhampton, Hampshire. Master's Mate 1804. Lieutenant 1805. Hills was a precise and careful officer and valued for his attention to detail. At Trafalgar Captain Hardy selected Hills to convey the news of Nelson injury to Adniral Lord Collingwood, for it was important for the Admiral to be aware of the injury to the Commander-in-Chief. Hills took the only undamaged boat left on *Victory* and was rowed to the *Royal Sovereign*, climbing aboard he noticed Collingwood had a leg bandaged from a battle wound. Hills gave his report, the Admiral enquired if Nelson's wound was dangerous, Hills hesitated then said he hoped it was not, the manner of this reply alerted Collingwood to the seriousness of the affair. Alexander Hills last entry in the Navy List was 1809.

KING Andrew, Lieutenant. Born 1778. Midshipman 1794. Lieutenant 1797. He served on *Desiree* at Copenhagen in 1801, where he was wounded. At Trafalgar he was rated as Fourth Lieutenant on the *Victory*, for his gallantry in that action he was promoted Commander in 1806. At Nelson's funeral he was one of the supporters to the bearer of the Banner of Emblems. Captain 1807. Commanded *Hebe* in the Copenhagen expedition of 1807. C.B 1831. He was Superintendent of the Packet Establishment at Falmouth, he died in 1835 whilst serving in that post.

LANCASTER Henry, Boy 1st class. Born at Wimbledon 1791. Son of Rev.Thomas Lancaster, Rector of Merton, Surrey. Lancaster as a 14 year old, was taken by his father to the naval dockyard at Portsmouth, it was his intention that the lad should serve as a First Class Volunteer on the *Victory*. The Rev. Lancaster of Merton was well known to Lord Nelson, an arrangement had been agreed between them earlier for the lad to serve on *Victory*. Lancaster was accepted as a trainee officer on board the flagship. For his services at Trafalgar, he was promoted to Midshipman in 1806. In 1813 Lancaster served on shore at the siege of Trieste, during which he suffered wounds, his action gained him promotion to Lieutenant. It is noted that on two separate ocassions he jumped into the sea from the *Apollo* to save the lives of seamen. Commander 1851. Died at Connaught Square, Hyde Park in 1862

LYONS John, Midshipman. Born 1783 in London. Son of John Lyons of Antigua and Lymington, Hampshire. His younger brother was Admiral Edmund Lyons, G.C.B. John Lyons entered service in 1798. Served on *St. George* at Copenhagen 1801. Whilst serving on the 74-gun *Magnificent* off Brest, the ship struck rocks and was wrecked, the crew were saved, but one cutter carrying over 60 men was captured by the French. Lyons transferred from *Tigre* on the 5th of October 1805 to *Victory*. At Trafalgar, his gallant conduct noted. On the return to England he joined *Queen*, the flagship of Admiral Lord Collingwood, who on 24th December 1805, promoted Lyons to Lieutenant. He served on *Eagle* at the reduction of Capri in August 1806. In 1810 he served on *Montague* at the reduction of St. Maura. Promoted Commander in 1814. Captain in 1830. He retired in 1851. Retired Rear-Admiral 1855. Retired Vice-Admiral 1862. Retired Admiral 1866. He died 1872.

NEVILL Ralph, Hon. AB (Supernumary). Born 1786 at Sion Hill, Middlesex. The son of the 2nd Earl of Abergavenny. Rated as AB on *Victory* for Trafalgar, aged 21 years, this being his second appearance on *Victory*. Had previously served on *Victory*, then discharged and sent away on duty, at that time he had appeared in the Muster Table, muster number 672, rated as Midshipman, aged 17. After Trafalgar in 1806, he was promoted to Lieutenant. Promoted Commander in 1808. In 1809 he commanded the brig *Actaeon* and assisted in the capture of the French privateer *Le Lezard*. The following year he was serving at the reduction of Mauritius. Captain 1811. Died in Boulogne in 1826.

OGILVIE David, Midshipman. Born 1782 in London. Served as Midshipman on *Victory* at Trafalgar. In January 1806, Ogilvie was transferred to *Queen*, flagship of Admiral Lord Collingwood. Promoted to Lieutenant in 1806, this for his gallant services during the Battle of Trafalgar.

PALMER Alexander, Midshipman. Born 1783 in London. Was killed from wounds received in the action at Trafalgar. Joined *Victory* as AB from *Queen* in May 1805. Entered in *Victory's* Muster Table as AB, with promotion to Midshipman made effective from 5th of August 1805. Died of his wounds on 28th October 1805, the last battle casualty to die on board ship.

PASCO John, Lieutenant of Signals. Born 1774 in the county of Devon. Entered service in 1784 as Captain's servant on the 32-gun *Druid*, although he was rated as an AB. He was promoted to Midshipman 1790, and Lieutenant in 1795. Pasco joined *Victory* in April 1803. At Trafalgar although the most senior of the nine lieutenants on *Victory*, Nelson selected Pasco for the duties of the Signal Lieutenant, with John Quilliam having the luck to be rated as the First Lieutenant. Pasco gained his place in naval history for the part he played in drafting Nelson's famous signal to the Fleet. On the 21st October at about 11.45am, Nelson turned to Pasco and said, "I wish to say to the Fleet: *England confides that every man will do his duty*". As it was required that this signal to be sent in the upmost haste, Pasco replied: "If your Lordship will permit me to substitute Expects for Confides, the signal will soon be completed, because the word Expects is in the vocabulary, and Confides must be spelt." Nelson replied: "That will do, Pasco, make it immediately." So the signal was sent: ENGLAND EXPECTS THAT EVERY MAN WILL DO HIS DUTY. As the Signal Lieutenant, Pasco was top side and exposed to much enemy fire, he was severely wounded by grape-shot in his right side and arm, for which he received a grant from the Patriotic Fund, of £100, and a pension from the Admiralty of £250 per year. For his action at Trafagar he was promoted Commander immediately. Captain 1811. Selected by the Admiralty to be Captain of *Victory* in 1847, the year he claimed his NGS medal with two clasps. Retired Rear-Admiral, 1847. Died at Stonehouse, Devonport, November 1853, aged 79.

PEAKE James Godwin, 1st Lieutenant RM. Born 1779 at Stafford. Entered the Marines at Chatham Division in 1796 as 2nd Lieutenant. Promoted to Lieutenant in 1799. Joined *Victory* April 1803 as second in command of the Marines detachment. When during the Trafalgar action Captain Adair was struck down, Peake who had been slightly wounded previously, took command of the Marines. At Nelson's funeral Lieutenant Peake was given the honour of being one of the pall bearers. Promoted Captain of Marines 1808. Peake was tragically drowned in company with a fellow officer, when a ship's boat turned over off the coast of Bermuda in 1809.

POAD James, Midshipman. Born 1789 at Devonport. Entered Royal Navy in 1803 as Third Class Volunteer on *Conqeror* under Captain Israel Pellew. Midshipman 1804. Joined *Victory* April 1805, being the youngest of the Midshipmen to serve on *Victory* at Trafalgar. Poad attended Nelson's funeral as one of the supporters of his banner as Knight of the Bath. His next ship was the 98 gun *Ocean*, flagship of Admiral Lord Collingwood, serving in the Mediterraenean. Poad was promoted Lieutenant in 1812, then paid off in November 1814. In 1829 he was appointed Agent for Transports Afloat. In this capacity Poad survived a shipwreck in 1830, whilst transporting troops of the 90th Regiment off the coast of Sicily. All 320 men of this Scottish Regiment plus 40 accompaning women and children were saved. In 1837 Poad was land based, this time in charge of semaphore stations, he was still serving in this capacity when he claimed his NGS medal in 1847. Greenwich Hospital Pension 1853. Promoted Retired Commander in 1855. Died in 1858.

POLLARD John, Midshipman. Born 1787 at Cawsand, Cornwall. Entered service in 1797. Signal-Midshipman on *Victory* at Trafalgar. During the action he was slightly wounded in arm by a splinter of wood. Whilst on the after part of the poop, he noticed a hail of musket shots hitting the poop and quarter deck, this was coming from soldiers crouching in the French tops. Pollard immediately took up a musket, and with Quarter Master John King acting as loader from barrels of ball-cartridges, Pollard kept up continuous fire upon the soldiers in the mizzen top of *Redoubtable*. It was these same French marksmen who were thought to be responsible for the death of Lord Nelson. Pollard's avenging fusillade of shots were successful in containing the enemy fire, unfortunately John King his loader was shot through the forehead and died instantly. Pollard was promoted Lieutenant in 1806. Saw service in the *Brunswick*, 1807, during which time he was involved in the capture of a Danish brig and cutter. From August 1836 he was in charge of a Coast Guard station. Greenwhich Hospital Pension 1853. Retired as Commander in 1864. Died in 1868 aged 81 years.

QUILLIAM John, 1st Lieutenant. Born 1771 on the Isle of Man. Unusual for a future officer he started his naval career as a pressed man from the lower deck. Lieutenant 1798. In 1799 he served as Third Lieutenant of the 38-gun *Ethalion* at the capture of the treasure ship *Thetis*, this ship was carrying bullion to the value of nearly $1.4 million. Quilliam's prize money for that days work was over £5,000, making him a very rich officer. Served on the 38-gun *Amazon* at Copenhagen 1801, was the only surviving officer of the ship, all had suffered as casualties in this bloody action, leaving Quilliam to take command of the *Amazon*. At Trafalgar his luck again was extraordinary, Nelson appointed him the First Lieutenant, ahead of the other eight lieutenants. After Trafalgar, as customary the First Lieutenant was immediately promoted, thus Quilliam was made Post Captain in November 1805. His first command was the bomb vessel *Aetna*. Later as Captain of the 36-gun *Crescent*, he captured an American privateer in 1813. Died in retirement on the Isle of Man in 1839.

RAM William Alexander, Lieutenant. Born 1784 in County Wexford, Ireland. Son of Lieutenant-Colonel Abel Ram, M.P., Wexford Militia. Lieutenant 1805. Joined *Victory* April 1805. Ram was killed by a deflected round shot from the *Redoubtable*, the shot passed upwards through the quarter deck causing a mass of splintered planking to hit those seamen and marines positioned near the gangway, one of those killed outright was Midshipman Robert Smith from Watford, the only man killed at Trafalgar to be awarded the NGS medal in 1848. Lieutenant Ram with multiple injuries was taken to the cockpit, the surgeon applied a tourniquet to stop the bleeding, but for some reason Ram removed the surgeon's tourniquet and very quickly bled to death. He was buried at sea, (thrown overboard) during the turmoil of the battle. Several days later his body was washed up on the Spanish coast, found by some English prisoners of war, who identified Ram's body by his clothes. The prisoners obtained permission from the Governor of Cadiz, to give Ram's body a Christian burial at Cadiz.

RANDALL William, Boy 1st class. Born 1788 in London. Joined *Victory* when she recommisioned at Chatham in May 1803. He served at Trafalgar as a Boy 1st class, after the action he was rewarded by promotion to Midshipman in 1806. In this same year he joined the 98-gun *Ocean*, with many of the crew he knew from *Victory*. Promoted Lieutenant in 1810. Not seen in the Navy List after 1814.

RANDALL/RANDLE Thomas, AB. Born in 1773 near Exeter. Joined the *Victory* May 1803, his name was entered as Randall with the rate of AB. He has a grave stone in the churchyard of the Topsham Parish Church, this gives his date of death as 2nd January 1851, aged 78 years.

REEVES Lewis Buckle, Second Lieutenant RM. Born 1786 in East Meon, Hampshire. Son of Thomas Reeves, whose family were originally from Bessborough, Killimer, County Clare, Ireland. Joined *Victory* August 1804. Was badly wounded by a deck shot during the Battle of Trafalgar, receiving a grant from the Lloyd's Patriotic Fund of £50. Promoted Lieutenant in 1807. Present at the defeat of the French at Babagne, near St. Louis in 1809. Retired on half-pay 1817. Died at Douglas, Isle of Man, 1861, aged 75 years.

REYNOLDS/MOSER Peter, AB. Born 1772 in Whitechapel, London. Volunteered for the Royal Navy July 1794. Joined *Saturn* as an AB, being transferred on 25th November 1794 to *Brunswick*. His ship served under Admiral Cornwallis, in the fighting withdrawl and repulse of the vastly superior French Fleet, 17 June 1795. In March 1797 Reynolds was promoted to Quarter Gunner and transfered to *Spencer* on 27 August 1800. He fought at the Gut of Gibraltar, 12th July 1801. Joined *Victory* on 11th May 1803. At Trafalgar he fought at his gun with much gallantry. After 19 years service in the Royal Navy he was discharged from *Milford*. He was admitted to Greenwich Hospital on 22nd July

1826, using the name Peter Moser. In 1831 he was promoted Boatswain to do duty in the Hospital wards. He died at Greenwich on 21st August 1856.

RIVERS William, Midshipman. Born 1788 at Portsea. Entered the Royal Navy in 1795 as a First Class Volunteer, aged seven. Served on *Victory* in Lord Hotham's action of 1795. Midshipman in 1796. With *Victory* in the Battle of St. Vincent 1797. Served on *Victory* as Midshipman at Trafalgar, during the action was severly wounded by round shot, had his left leg amputated by the surgeons. Promoted Lieutenant in January 1806. Awarded £80 for his injuries by Lloyd's Patriotic Fund. Received a pension from the Admiralty of £91.5s.0d. per annum. Lieutenant in the Cossack in the expedition to Copenhagen in 1807. Served as First Lieutenant in the *Cretan* for the Walcheren expedition of 1809. Warden at Woolwich Dockyard 1824-26. Lieutenant of Greenwich Hospital 1826. Died at Greenwich Hospital 1856. Rivers submitted a claim for the 'Copenhagen 1807' clasp to his NGS medal. His application was accepted and listed together with 204 other names, all men who were serving in Lord Gambier's attack on Copenhagen. The Admiralty decided against awarding a clasp to the Naval General Service Medal for this action.

ROBINS Thomas Lowton, Master's Mate. Born 1787 at Portsmouth. Entered the Royal Navy in 1798 as a First Class Volunteer. Served in the brig *Teazer* in an expedition to Holland 1799, served on this ship at Copenhagen 1801. Joined *Victory* in 1803 as a Midshipman. Promoted to Master's Mate on 30th June 1805. His gallant conduct during the Battle of Trafalgar gained him immediate promotion to Lieutenant. Served in the 32-gun *Pallas* in an attack against the 40-gun *La Minerve* under the batteries on Isle d'Aix, 1808. Served in the Walcheren expedition 1809. Also destroyed ships in the Basque Roads, 1809. Taken prisoner when his ship *Manilla* was wrecked off the Haak Sand near Texel, he served 30 months in prison at Verdun. Commander 1821. Captain 1851. Died 1852. NGS medal with four clasps.

ROBERTS Richard Francis, Midshipman. Born 1785 at Burton Bradstock, Dorset. Son of Richard Roberts who was a close friend of Captain Hardy. Joined *Victory* as an AB in September 1805, promoted to Midshipman on 19th October 1805. After Trafalgar he joined *Ocean* in January 1806 with other members of *Victory's* crew. He decided to leave the navy early in December 1806.

ROBERTSON/WALKER James, Midshipman. Born 1783 at Stornoway, Scotland. Son of James Robertson, D.L., J.P., of Stornoway. Entered service in 1801 as AB on the sloop *Inspector*, within weeks he was promoted to Midshipman. Served in *Canopus* 1803-04. Joined *Victory* as Midshipman, fought with distinction in the thick of the action during the Battle of Trafalgar. Was promoted to Master's Mate in November 1805. Lieutenant 1808. Commander 1815. In 1824 Robertson married Anne Walker and assumed the name James Robertson Walker. Reserve Captain 1851. Died in 1858, buried at Distington, Cumbria.

ROME John, LM. Born 1782 in Battersea, London. Working the River Thames as a lighterman, John Rome was grabbed by the naval press gang in early 1803. Sent to the *Victory* on 11th May 1803, because of his ability he was placed on the signal staff of the flag ship. At Trafalgar it was his duty to raise the signals, it fell to John Rome to assemble and hoist Lord Nelson's historic signal "England expects etc . ." After Trafalgar and the return of *Victory's* to Chatham, it was known the crew would possibly be drafted to *Ocean*. Rome knew he would be sent off to sea for an indefinite period of service, so he decided to desert and return to London. Many years later in 1845, a gentleman found John Rome hawking watercress in the streets of Blackfriars, London. During a conversation he learned of this old sailor's past, as Rome was obviously destitute and in poor health , the gentleman Mr.Chevers who had been a Surgeon on *Tonnant* at Trafalgar, wrote to John Pasco asking for his help. Captain John Pasco used his influence with the Admiralty. Their Lordships made an exception and overlooked the earlier desertion by Rome, he was accepted as a Greenwich Naval Hospital pensioner. He died there in 1860, aged 78 years.

ROTELY Lewis, Second Lieutenant RM. Born 1785 at Neath, Glamorgan. Entered the Royal Marines as a Second Lieutenant in 1805. Joined *Victory* in September 1805, serving through the battle with distinction. Promoted Lieutenant in 1808. He served on *Cleopatra* at the capture of Martinique in 1809. In the same year, he commanded a detachment of marines at the capture of Guadaloupe. He is on record as having saved four persons from drowning. Retired on full pay, 1814. The Rotely Scholarship at the Royal Naval School, Eltham, was founded in his memory. Died at May Hill, Swansea in 1861.

SCOTT Rev. Alexander John, Chaplain. Born 1768 at Rotherhithe, London. Ordained in 1792. Chaplain R.N. 1793. Private Secretary to Admiral Sir Hyde Parker, 1795-1801. Chaplain on *London* at Copenhagen 1801. Chaplain on *Victory* at Trafalgar. Private and confidential secretary to Lord Nelson 1803-05. Scott's linguistic ability in French, Spanish, Italian and other languages, was most useful to Nelson, translating documents and orders taken from prizes, he would gain foreign intelligence and arrange documents of surrender. Scott was a constant companion of Nelson and would at times be invited to dine with him. In the cockpit he attended the dying Nelson throughout his ordeal, giving him comfort and light drinks. He considered it his duty to watch over the corpse every night as it lay in state at Greenwich. Appointed D.D. by Royal Mandate 1806. Died at Ecclesfield Vicarage, near Sheffield in 1840.

SCOTT John, Admiral's Secretary. Born 1768. Purser of the 100-gun *Royal Sovereign*. Scott was appointed to the *Victory* as Secretary to Lord Nelson in 1803. At Trafalgar he was on the quarter deck, when at the start of the battle, he was struck by a round shot, this shot all but cut his body in two, his remains were immediately thrown over the side, but not before Lord Nelson had spotted the sad affair, he turned and asked,"*Is that poor Scott?*" John Scott had endeared himself to the Admiral by his hard work and modest manner, so it was a blow to Nelson to lose such a trusted servant.

SIBBALD James, Midshipman. Born 1786 at Leith, Edinburgh. Midshipman on the *Defiance*. Transferred to *Victory* on 14th September 1805. The following day the *Victory* was ordered to sail, Lord Nelson was eager to seek out the enemy and bring them to action. At Trafalgar, Sibbald service in the battle was noted, he was promoted in the first week of November 1805, to Master's Mate. Promoted Commander 1814. Died at Edinburgh in 1843.

SMITH Neil, Assistant Surgeon. Joined *Victory* in January 1805 as First Assistant Surgeon. Served through the Trafalgar action with distinction, he was commended for his dedicated service to the wounded and dying. Was rewarded with promotion to Surgeon in 1806. Died in 1819. He appears in the painting "The Death of Nelson", by Arthur William Devis. Neil Smith also appears in the painting by Benjamin West, showing Nelson fatally wounded on the deck of *Victory*, he is depicted immediately beside Lord Nelson .

SMITH Robert, Midshipman. Born 1786 at Watford, Hertfordshire. As a Midshipman Robert Smith joined *Victory* on 19th May 1803. At Trafalgar, Smith was killed when a round shot came upwards through the quarter deck, near the gangway, sending a mass of splintered planking hurtling amongst the seamen and marines. In this same incident Lieutenant Ram was fatally wounded. Robert Smith's remains were thrown over the side during the action. Captain Hardy had him entered in the muster table as "DD", killed in action. Yet in 1848, a claim for the "Naval War Medal" was submitted by someone, and approved by the Admiralty. The NGS medal with clasp Trafalgar was forwarded to the Smith family at Watford. Making this the only NGS medal to a man killed at Trafalgar.

SPENCER Samuel, Master's Mate. Born 1779 in Halifax, Nova Scotia. Entered service in 1796. Midshipman 1797 in the *Active* during the operations off the coast of Egypt in 1801. Promoted Master's Mate in 1803. Served on the *Maidstone* when he was wounded during the pursuit of a French privateer. Also in boat service against a French convoy at La Vandour 1804. Joined *Victory* in August 1804, as Master's Mate. his service at Trafalgar gained him promotion to Lieutenent in 1806. He saw further service with the *Queen* off Cadiz. Transferred to *Prince of Wales* serving in home waters. Later in the Transport Service. Then acted as Admiralty Agent on a mail vessel. Died at Birkenhead, Cheshire, December 1850, aged 71 years.

SYMONS William Henry, Master's Mate. Born 1782 at Ashford, Kent. Entered service in 1797. Served in *Canada* at the defeat of the French squadron under the command of Commodore Bompart, the intention of the French squadron was the invasion of Ireland. Served at Trafalgar with distinction and was promoted to Lieutenant immediately on cessation of the battle. Retired Commander 1842. Died at Plymouth in November 1851.

TARRANT/TERRANT William, Quarter Gunner. Born 1780 on the Isle of Wight. Tarrant joined *Victory* in May 1803. Served at Trafalgar with the rank of Quarter Gunner. Later gained promotion to Boatswain. In June 1977, the decendants of William Tarrant wrote to the Commanding Officer of *Victory* at Portsmouth, to inform him that the Naval General Service Medal clasp Trafalgar, awarded to William Tarrant was still in the possesion of the family.

THOVEZ Philip, Midshipman. Born 1785 in Naples, Italy. Entered service on the *Victory*, 4th October 1804, mustered as AB, promoted on 1st June 1805 to Midshipman. When *Victory* was paid off January 1806, Thovez joined the 98 gun *Ocean*. He was to serve alongside many of the ex-crew of Nelson's old flagship. Listed as a Purser in the Royal Navy with the a Warrant date of 1809. It is thought he died in 1840.

WESTERBURGH William, Surgeon's Mate. Joined *Victory* on 16th of March 1805, the day his warrant granted him the rank of Surgeon's Second Mate. At Trafalgar he was worked hard in the cockpit attending the many battle wounded. He is recorded in the painting of Benjamin West, showing Lord Nelson surrounded by his officers and men on the deck of the flagship, just after he had been struck by a French musket ball. William Westerburgh is pictured in the group close beside Lord Nelson.

WESTPHAL George Augustus, Midshipman. Born 1785 at Lambeth, London. Westphal was from an ancient German titled family, decended from the Counts Westphal. He joined the Royal Navy under the patronage of the Duke of Kent, he had an elder brother Philip who by the same patronage was already serving in the Royal Navy. George Westphal entered service in 1798, as a First Class Volunteer on the 24-gun *Porcupine*. Joined *Victory* on 31st July 1803. During the Battle of Trafalgar Westphal was wounded in the head, he was taken to the cockpit and laid close by Lord Nelson. His head wound bled so profusely that one of the attendants folded up Lord Nelson's coat to make a pillow for the Midshipman's head, the blood soaked into the coat causing a portion of the cloth to stick to his wound, later it had to be cut from his head; this small section of Nelson's coat was kept by Westphal as a treasured momento. In the first week of November 1805, he gained promotion to Master's Mate. In August 1806, Westphal was promoted to Lieutenant. In 1807 whilst being invalided home in a merchant ship, he was wounded and captured by a French privateer, taken to Guadaloupe and held in a prison ship, he escaped by small boat and was picked up by an American schooner, which in turn was boarded by an English privateer who landed this escaped officer in Antigua, ready for passage to England. Lieutenant of *Belleisle* on shore at the reduction of Martinique in 1809. Lieutenant of *Marlborough* in Chesapeake Bay, here he commanded the boats of the squadron, he was wounded during the action, for his gallantry he was promoted Commander in 1813. Captain 1819. Knighted in 1824. Flag Captain to Admiral Sir George Cockburn on North American Station 1832-34. Rear-Admiral 1851. Vice-Admiral 1857. Admiral 1863. Westphal died at Hove in 1875.

WHIPPLE Thomas, Captain's Clerk. Born 1785 in Devon. Captain Hardy transferred from the *Amphion* to *Victory* on the 31st of July 1803, at this transfer Hardy had his clerk Thomas Whipple accompanied him to *Victory*. During the Battle of Trafalgar, Whipple was talking with Midshipman George Westphal when a round-shot narrowly missed the two of them, it passed so close that the pressure from the large shot killed Whipple outright, he died without it leaving so much as a mark or bruise on his body. A phenomenon that is understood today, but at the time it caused much speculation.

WILLIAMS Edward, Lieutenant. Born in Dorset. Lieutenant 1796. Joined *Victory* on 25 January 1804, served at the Battle of Trafalgar with distinction, promoted Commander in November 1805. At Nelson's funeral he was one of the lieutenants of *Victory* to carry a bannerol of lineage. He was Commander of Greenwich Hospital in 1840. Williams died in 1843.

WILLMET William, Boatswain. Promoted to Boatswain with warrant dated 14 March 1803. Entered service on *Victory* 29th of March 1805. During the Battle of Trafalgar he was noted for his distinguished service in the action. Willmet was slightly wounded by gunshot in the thigh, he refused to leave his station and present himself to the surgeons, he bound the wound himself. It is said he insisted that he might be allowed to stay at his station for the duration of the fight. Lloyd's Patriotic Fund awarded Boatswain Willmet £30 for his injuries

YULE John, Lieutenant. Born 1778 at Plymouth. Served as Midshipman under Admiral Sir William Cornwallis during his fighting withdrawl from the superior French fleet off Brest in June 1795. Promoted Lieutenant 1797. First Lieutenant of *Alexander* at the Battle of the Nile 1798. Served as Lieutenant on *Victory* at Trafalgar, for his service during the battle Yule was promoted Commander 1805. At Nelson's funeral 1806, he carried the bannerol of lineage. Received a Greenwich Hospital pension in 1835. Died at Plymouth in 1840.

SOME WHO CLAIMED TO HAVE SERVED ON VICTORY AT TRAFALGAR

PROWSE William, Captain of *HMS Sirius*. Stated to have been requested to attend a meeting with Nelson on board *Victory* just prior to the battle, but owing to commencement of the action, he had trouble in returning to his ship the *Sirius*. Prowse claims to have been on *Victory* during the battle.

JOHNSON W. W. Percival, Midshipman later Admiral. Stated he had served on *Victory* at Trafalgar. A claim to this effect was published in "The Graphic" of 1st March 1879, pages 216-217. He appears in an engraving entitled "The surviving officers of the Battle of Trafalgar. Fought Oct. 21, 1805." Admiral Johnson is shown seated with six other officers, all whom had served at Trafalgar. A caption immediately below reads: "Admiral W. W. Percival Johnson, 1st Class Volunteer *HMS Childers*; Guest on Board the *Victory*." But his memory must have failed him, because as a Midshipman he had transferred from *Victory* to *Eurydice* on the 12th October 1805. The 24-gun *Eurydice* did not serve at Trafalgar, at the time of the battle she was detached to stop and search shiping along the coast.

SALTER Daniel, Midshipman. Arrived on *Victory* from Gibraltar after Trafalgar. His appearance on board was entered in the Muster Table with the date 29th October 1805. Muster number 981.

REFERENCES

Victory's Muster Table, 9th September to 31st October 1805. ADM 36-15900.

Naval Hospital Ledger, Gibraltar. ADM 102/232.

Third Report of the Committee for Managing the Patriotic Fund. Lloyd's Patriotic Fund Report 1806.

The Sheerness Letter Book. Public Records Office, Kew. WO 292/1.

The London Gazette, Extraordinary. Wednesday November 27, 1805.

Steel's, Haultain's, Allen's and Lean's Navy Lists.

Admiralty Office, Royal Marine List. S. Brooke, Paternoster Row

O'Byrnes Naval Biography, 1849.

Marshall's Naval Biography, volumes 1823 to 1835.

The Naval History of Great Britain by William James, 1886, vols. 1-6.

The Men who fought with Nelson in HMS Victory at Trafalgar. Lt. Cdr. C.P. Addis.

Information on The Patriotic Fund swords, taken from details of the late Peter Dale collection.

The Fell papers. Royal Naval Museum, Portsmouth.

The Life of Admiral Lord Nelson from his Lordship's manuscripts. Clarke & McArthur, 1809.

The Trafalgar Roll , R. H. Mackenzie, 1913

History of Kingston-upon-Hull. J. J. Sheeham, 1864.

ACKNOWLEDGEMENTS

My thanks are due to Lloyd's of London for their kind assistance with details of recipients of the Lloyd's Patriotic Fund Awards, and for allowing me to reproduce photographs from their fine collection of Patriotic Fund Awards.

My sincere thanks to Mrs. P. Douglas-Morris for her kindness in allowing me to use illustrations from the Captain Douglas-Morris collection.

National Maritime Museum, London, SE10 9NF. For the photo of the sinking of HMS Implacable.

Printed in the United Kingdom
by Lightning Source UK Ltd.
128860UK00001BA/11/A